THE RICH REALTOR'S PLAYBOOK: HOW TO OUTPERFORMING THE COMPETITION IN REAL ESTATE

Kwame Joseph

4K Book Publishing

To my beautiful wife, and truly incredible son & daughter

INTRODUCTION

As a real estate agent, building a repeat business is key to long-term success in the industry. Repeat business comes from clients who trust you, who appreciate your expertise, and who know you have their best interests at heart. It's a powerful way to build a sustainable business, because it generates a steady stream of referrals and leads.

But building a repeat business isn't just about making more money. It's about building a reputation as a trusted and respected realtor who cares deeply about their clients and their needs. When you focus on building a repeat business, you're investing in relationships that can last a lifetime.

To build a repeat business, you need to go above and beyond to exceed your clients' expectations. This means providing exceptional customer service, listening carefully to their needs and concerns, and being responsive and communicative throughout the buying or selling process. It means building a strong brand and marketing yourself effectively, so that clients know who you are and what you stand for.

But building a repeat business isn't just about the individual realtor. It's about the industry as a whole. When real estate professionals focus on building repeat business, they raise the bar for the entire industry. They create a culture of excellence, where the standard is not just to sell houses, but to build relationships that last.

Of course, building a repeat business is only part of the equation. To truly stand out as a realtor, you need to develop expertise in a particular niche or market, provide outstanding customer service, and stay up-to-date on industry trends and changes. You need to network and get involved in the community, building a strong network of industry contacts and making a positive impact in the world around you.

Being a standout realtor is about much more than just making sales. It's about building relationships, providing exceptional service, and making a positive impact in the world around you. It's about being a trusted advisor and a respected member of the community. And when you focus on these things, the business will follow.

When it comes to real estate, being a standout realtor is critical to success. There are many realtors out there, and the competition can be fierce. That's why it's so important to differentiate yourself from the crowd by providing exceptional service, developing expertise in a particular area, and building a strong brand.

Building a repeat business is one of the most effective ways to stand out as a realtor. Repeat business comes from clients who trust you, who appreciate your expertise, and who know you have their best interests at heart. It's a powerful way to build a sustainable business, because it generates a steady stream of referrals and leads.

To build a repeat business, you need to prioritize the needs and concerns of your clients above all else. You need to be responsive, communicative, and proactive in helping them navigate the buying or selling process. This means staying in touch with past clients, asking for referrals, and going above and beyond to exceed expectations.

But building a repeat business isn't just about making more money. It's about building a reputation as a trusted and respected realtor who cares deeply about their clients and their needs. When you focus on building a repeat business, you're investing in relationships that can last a lifetime.

To truly stand out as a realtor, you also need to develop expertise in a particular area. This could mean specializing in luxury homes, first-time buyers, or a particular geographic area. When you become known as an expert in a particular area, clients will seek you out and trust your advice.

Marketing and branding are also key to standing out as a realtor. You need to build a strong brand and market yourself effectively, so that clients know who you are and what you stand for. This means creating a memorable logo and tagline, having a strong online presence, and leveraging social media to reach potential clients.

Networking and community involvement are also critical to standing out as a realtor. By building a strong network of industry contacts and getting involved in the community, you can make a positive impact and build your reputation as a trusted advisor.

In conclusion, being a standout realtor is about much more than just making sales. It's about building relationships, providing exceptional service, developing expertise, building a strong brand, and making a positive impact in the world around you. When you focus on these things, the business will follow, and you'll be well on your way to a successful career in real estate.

magna aliqua. Ut enim ad minim veniam, quis nostrud exercitation ullamco laboris.

PROLOGUE

Step into the world of real estate where fortunes are made, dreams are realized, and the competition is fierce. In this realm, a select few rise above the rest, wielding a playbook filled with secrets to outperforming the competition and achieving remarkable success. Welcome to "The Rich Realtor's Playbook."

Within these pages lies the key to unlocking your true potential in the cutthroat world of real estate. Whether you're a seasoned professional or just starting your journey, this playbook will equip you with the strategies, mindset, and skills necessary to stand out from the crowd and dominate your market.

Through captivating stories, practical techniques, and expert advice, we unveil the secrets of the "Rich Realtors." Learn how to attract clients like a magnet, build an unshakable brand, deliver exceptional customer service, and negotiate with finesse.

But this playbook is not just about winning transactions; it's about transforming your career and your life. It's about embracing a mindset of excellence, pushing the boundaries, and rewriting the rules of real estate.

So, get ready to take a leap into the extraordinary. "The Rich Realtor's Playbook" is your ticket to outperforming the competition, exceeding expectations, and becoming a true industry leader. It's time to claim your place among the elite. Are you ready?

trud exercitation ullamco laboris.

THE RICH REALTOR'S PLAYBOOK: HOW TO OUTPERFORMING THE COMPETITION IN REAL ESTATE

By Kwame Joseph

CHAPTER 1: BUILDING A REPEAT BUSINESS

As a real estate agent, building a repeat business is one of the most important things you can do to ensure long-term success in the industry. Repeat business is the result of satisfied clients who trust you, appreciate your expertise, and know that you have their best interests at heart. It is a powerful way to build a sustainable business, generating a steady stream of referrals and leads.

But why is repeat business so important? For one, it is more cost-effective than constantly having to find new clients. It is also a testament to your abilities as a realtor and your commitment to providing exceptional service. By focusing on building a repeat business, you are investing in relationships that can last a lifetime.

There are several strategies you can employ to generate repeat business. One of the most important is to stay in touch with past clients. This can be done through regular phone calls, emails, or newsletters. By staying in touch, you demonstrate that you care about your clients beyond the transaction and are invested in their long-term success.

Another important strategy is to provide exceptional service. This means going above and beyond to exceed your clients' expectations, being responsive and communicative throughout the buying or selling process, and prioritizing their needs and concerns above all else. By providing exceptional service, you create a positive experience that clients will remember and want to repeat.

Asking for referrals is also a critical component of generating repeat business. Here are the top 10 best ways to ask for referrals and generate new business from existing clients:

1. Ask directly: The most effective way to ask for referrals is to simply ask directly. Let your clients know that you would appreciate any referrals they can provide.
2. Host a client appreciation event: Show your appreciation for your clients by hosting an event in their honor. This can be a great way to generate referrals while also building relationships.
3. Offer incentives: Consider offering incentives such as discounts or gift cards for referrals.
4. Follow up: After a successful transaction, follow up with your clients to thank them and ask for referrals.
5. Provide exceptional service: As mentioned earlier, providing exceptional service is key to generating referrals.
6. Stay in touch: By staying in touch with past clients, you can stay top-of-mind and generate referrals.
7. Showcase your expertise: By showcasing your expertise in a particular area, you can attract clients who are looking for someone with your level of knowledge and experience.
8. Use social media: Social media can be a powerful tool for generating referrals. Share your successes and ask for referrals from your followers.
9. Partner with other professionals: Partnering with other professionals such as mortgage brokers or home inspectors can help generate referrals.
10. Be persistent: Don't be afraid to ask for referrals multiple times. Persistence can pay off in the long run.

Building a repeat business is critical to long-term success as a real estate agent. By staying in touch with past clients, providing exceptional service, and asking for referrals, you can create a steady stream of business that will sustain your career for years to come. Remember, building a repeat business is not just about making more money, it's about building relationships that can last a lifetime.

Trust is one of the most important elements in establishing repeat business for a real estate agent. When clients trust their agent, they are more likely to refer them to others and use their services again in the future. Trust is built over time, through consistent actions that demonstrate integrity, honesty, and a commitment to the client's best interests.

One reason why trust is so important is because buying or selling a home is a significant financial transaction that requires a great deal of trust in the agent. Clients need to feel confident that their agent is acting in their best interest and providing them with accurate information and advice. If a client feels that their agent is not trustworthy, they will be less likely to use their services again or recommend them to others.

Another reason why trust is important is that it helps to establish a strong relationship between the agent and the client. When clients trust their agent, they are more likely to communicate openly and honestly about their needs and concerns. This allows the agent to better understand the client's goals and preferences, which can lead to a more successful transaction.

Trust is also important because it can help to differentiate an agent from their competitors. In a highly competitive industry such as real estate, trust can be a powerful differentiator that sets an agent apart from others. Clients are more likely to choose an agent that they trust, even if they charge slightly higher fees or have less experience than other agents.

Building trust with clients takes time and effort. It requires agents to consistently demonstrate their commitment to the client's best interests, provide accurate information, and communicate effectively. By doing so, they can establish a reputation as a trustworthy agent that clients will be happy to refer to others and use again in the future.

Trust is critical in establishing repeat business for a real estate agent. It helps to build strong relationships with clients, differentiate agents from competitors, and establish a reputation as a trustworthy and reliable professional. By focusing on building trust with clients, agents can establish a solid foundation for long-term success in the industry.

In the highly competitive world of real estate, providing exceptional service is a key strategy for building a repeat business. Exceptional service means going above and beyond to exceed your clients' expectations, being responsive and communicative throughout the buying or selling process, and prioritizing their needs and concerns above all else.

There are several reasons why providing exceptional service is so important. Firstly, it helps to establish a positive reputation for the agent. When clients receive exceptional service, they are more likely to tell others about their positive experience. This can lead to referrals and new business opportunities for the agent. On the other hand, if clients receive poor service, they are likely to share their negative experience with others, which can damage the agent's reputation and limit their ability to generate new business.

Secondly, providing exceptional service can help to create a positive experience for clients that they will remember and want to repeat. Buying or selling a home can be a stressful and emotional process, and agents who provide exceptional service can make the experience more enjoyable and less stressful for their clients. By prioritizing the client's needs and concerns and being responsive and communicative throughout the process, agents can create a sense of trust and confidence that can lead to repeat business in the future.

Thirdly, providing exceptional service can help agents to stand out from their competitors. In a crowded market, agents who provide exceptional service can differentiate themselves from others and establish themselves as trusted and reliable professionals. This can help to attract new clients and generate repeat business over time.

To provide exceptional service, agents need to be proactive in their approach. This means being responsive and communicative with clients throughout the buying or selling process, and anticipating their needs and concerns before they arise. Agents should also prioritize the client's needs and concerns above all else, and be willing to go above and beyond to exceed their expectations.

Providing exceptional service is a critical strategy for building a repeat business in the real estate industry. By prioritizing the client's needs and concerns, being responsive and communicative, and going above and beyond to exceed their expectations, agents can establish a positive reputation, create a positive experience for clients, and differentiate themselves from their competitors. By focusing on providing exceptional service, agents can build a loyal base of repeat clients that will help to sustain their business over the long term.

Staying in touch with past clients is crucial in building repeat business as a Realtor. When you maintain a relationship with clients after a successful transaction, you remain top-of-mind when they or someone they know needs real estate services in the future. This is why it is important to consistently communicate with clients even after the transaction has closed.

Staying in touch can take many forms, such as sending monthly newsletters, holiday cards, or simply checking in every so often. The key is to make sure that clients know you are still thinking about them and that you value their business. When clients feel appreciated and remembered, they are more likely to refer you to their friends and family.

Staying top-of-mind is also important because people may not need real estate services right away, but when they do, they are more likely to contact someone they have recently interacted with. By staying in touch, you are not only reminding clients of your services, but you are also building trust and rapport with them over time.

One effective way to stay top-of-mind is through social media. By maintaining a strong presence on platforms like Facebook, Twitter, and Instagram, you can engage with clients on a regular basis and share updates on the market or your business. This can be a great way to remind clients of your expertise and reinforce your brand in their minds.

Overall, staying in touch and staying top-of-mind are critical components of generating referrals and building repeat business as a Realtor. By consistently communicating with clients and maintaining a strong presence, you can ensure that you are the first person they think of when they or someone they know needs real estate services.As a realtor, it's essential to establish yourself as an expert in a particular area or niche. This can help you attract clients who are specifically looking for someone with your level of knowledge and experience. By showcasing your expertise in a particular area, you not only differentiate yourself from other realtors, but you also build trust and credibility with potential clients.

For example, if you specialize in luxury properties, you can showcase your expertise by highlighting your experience working with high-end buyers and sellers, sharing your knowledge of the local luxury market, and providing valuable insights on the latest trends and developments in the industry. This can help you establish yourself as a go-to resource for luxury real estate in your area, and attract clients who are specifically looking for someone with your level of expertise.

Similarly, if you specialize in a particular neighborhood or type of property, such as condos or single-family homes, you can use your expertise to differentiate yourself and attract clients who are looking for someone with specialized knowledge. By sharing your insights on the local market, providing data-driven analysis of the latest trends and developments, and showcasing your experience working with similar clients, you can establish yourself as an expert in your niche and build a loyal following of clients who trust your expertise.

Another way to showcase your expertise is through thought leadership and content marketing. By creating high-quality content, such as blog posts, videos, and social media posts, that demonstrate your knowledge and expertise, you can attract clients who are looking for someone with your level of insight and guidance. By consistently producing valuable content that helps educate and inform your audience, you can establish yourself as a trusted advisor and build long-term relationships with your clients.

Showcasing your expertise in a particular area or niche is critical to building a repeat business as a realtor. By establishing yourself as an expert, you can attract clients who are specifically looking for someone with your level of knowledge and experience, differentiate yourself from other realtors, and build trust and credibility with potential clients. Whether you specialize in luxury properties, a particular neighborhood, or a type of property, investing in your expertise can pay dividends in the form of a loyal client base and a thriving real estate business.

In today's world, social media has become an essential tool for realtors to build their brand and generate referrals. With over 3 billion people using social media, it has become a powerful platform to connect with potential clients, showcase properties, and build a loyal following. Social media is an excellent way to showcase your expertise, connect with your audience, and provide them with valuable information about the real estate industry.

Using social media, you can create content that resonates with your audience and highlights your expertise in the industry. This could be anything from sharing tips on home buying or selling, to showcasing a new listing or providing insights into the local real estate market. By sharing your successes and expertise, you can attract potential clients who are looking for a realtor with your level of knowledge and experience.

In addition to showcasing your expertise, social media is also an excellent platform to ask for referrals. Your followers are likely to have friends, family, or colleagues who may be in the market for a new home or looking to sell their current property. By asking for referrals and sharing your success stories, you are more likely to generate leads and build a strong referral network.

However, it's important to use social media strategically to build your brand and generate referrals. It's important to have a clear social media strategy that aligns with your overall business goals. This includes choosing the right platforms to focus on, creating engaging content that resonates with your audience, and consistently sharing updates and information.

Consistency is key when it comes to using social media for real estate. You want to ensure that you are staying top-of-mind with your followers by regularly sharing updates and engaging with them. This could be anything from responding to comments and messages, sharing content from other industry leaders, or hosting Q&A sessions to answer questions about the real estate market.

Another way to use social media to generate referrals is by leveraging your existing network. You can encourage your clients to follow you on social media and share your content with their own networks. By doing so, you are increasing the likelihood that your content will be seen by potential clients who are interested in working with you.

Social media is a powerful tool for realtors to build their brand and generate referrals. By showcasing your expertise, asking for referrals, and staying top-of-mind with your audience, you can attract new clients and build a loyal following. It's important to have a clear social media strategy that aligns with your business goals and to use social media consistently to build your brand and generate referrals.

Partnering with other professionals is a great way to generate referrals and build a repeat business as a Realtor. By working with other professionals such as mortgage brokers or home inspectors, you can establish a mutually beneficial relationship that can lead to increased business for both parties. Here are some reasons why partnering with other professionals is important:

1. Access to a wider network: Partnering with other professionals can provide you with access to their network of contacts and potential clients. By tapping into their network, you can expand your reach and generate more leads.
2. Expertise: Partnering with professionals who specialize in areas such as mortgages or home inspections can provide you with a level of expertise that you may not have. This can help you better serve your clients and provide them with a more comprehensive service.
3. Credibility: Partnering with other professionals can also add to your credibility as a Realtor. When you align yourself with reputable professionals, it can enhance your reputation and make potential clients more likely to trust you.
4. Referral opportunities: By partnering with other professionals, you can create referral opportunities for each other. For example, a mortgage broker may refer their clients to you

when they are ready to buy a home, and you can refer your clients to the mortgage broker for financing.

To make the most of your partnerships with other professionals, it's important to establish clear expectations and communication. You should also make sure that you are referring your clients to professionals who provide high-quality service and are a good fit for your clients' needs.

In addition to partnering with other professionals, you can also leverage their expertise to provide additional value to your clients. For example, if you partner with a home inspector, you can offer your clients a discounted home inspection as part of your service. This can help differentiate you from other Realtors and provide your clients with added value.

Overall, partnering with other professionals is an effective way to build a repeat business as a Realtor. By working together, you can generate more referrals, expand your network, and enhance your reputation in the industry.

When it comes to building a repeat business as a realtor, being persistent is key. It's important to not be afraid to ask for referrals multiple times and to be consistent in your approach. However, it's also important to be aware of the line between persistence and obnoxiousness.

Persistence can pay off in the long run, as potential clients may not always be ready to refer you right away. It's important to keep your name and brand in their minds and continue to remind them of the exceptional service you offer. This can be achieved through regular communication, such as email newsletters, phone calls, or even occasional drop-ins.

When asking for referrals, it's important to be direct and specific. Let your clients know that you value their opinion and would appreciate any referrals they may have. You can also provide incentives for referrals, such as a discount on their next transaction or a gift card.

However, it's also important to respect your clients' boundaries and not be overly aggressive in asking for referrals. Remember that your clients are busy people and may not always have the time or desire to refer you to others. By being respectful and understanding, you can maintain positive relationships with your clients and increase the likelihood of receiving referrals in the future.

Persistence also extends to following up with potential referrals. If a client has referred someone to you, it's important to follow up with them in a timely manner and provide exceptional service to the referred individual. This not only shows your commitment to your clients, but also reinforces the positive experience your clients had with you.

Persistence is an important component of building a repeat business as a realtor. By being direct and specific in asking for referrals, providing incentives, and following up with potential referrals, you can increase the likelihood of receiving referrals and ultimately, build a successful and thriving real estate business.

When it comes to building a repeat business as a realtor, being persistent is important. However, it's crucial to strike the right balance between being persistent and being harassing. Here are some tips on how to be persistent without crossing the line:

1. Be respectful of your clients' time and space: While it's important to follow up with clients, you don't want to come across as pushy or intrusive. Respect their boundaries and avoid bombarding them with phone calls, emails, or text messages.

2. Personalize your approach: Don't send the same generic message to all your clients. Instead, tailor your message to their specific needs and interests. This will show that you value their individuality and are genuinely interested in helping them.

3. Provide value: When you're reaching out to clients, make sure you're providing them with something of value. This could be useful information about the real estate market, tips for preparing their home for sale, or insights into the buying process. By providing value, you'll position yourself as a

helpful resource and increase the chances that they'll want to work with you again.

4. Follow up at appropriate times: While it's important to be persistent, you also need to be mindful of timing. For example, you wouldn't want to follow up with a client immediately after they've closed on a new home. Instead, wait a few weeks or months and then reach out to see how they're doing and if they know anyone who could benefit from your services.

5. Keep it professional: While you want to be friendly and approachable, it's important to maintain a professional demeanor. Avoid using slang or casual language, and make sure your communications are free of spelling and grammar errors.

By following these tips, you can be persistent without being harassing, and build a strong foundation for repeat business as a realtor.

CHAPTER 2: MARKETING AND BRANDING

Branding

Having a strong brand is essential to stand out in a crowded market and attract clients. Your brand represents who you are, what you stand for, and what clients can expect when they work with you. It's important to invest time and effort into building a strong brand that resonates with your target audience.

In the world of real estate, where competition is fierce and the market is constantly changing, having a strong brand is essential to stand out and attract clients. A strong brand is more than just a logo or tagline, it represents who you are, what you stand for, and what clients can expect when they work with you. Your brand is your reputation, and it's what sets you apart from the competition.

A strong brand can help you build trust and credibility with clients. When clients see a strong and consistent brand, they are more likely to trust that you are a reputable and reliable realtor who can deliver results. Your brand can also communicate what makes you unique and why clients should choose to work with you over other realtors.

Building a strong brand takes time and effort, but it's an investment that can pay off in the long run. To build a strong brand, you need to have a clear understanding of who your target audience is and what they are looking for in a realtor. You need to identify your unique selling points and communicate them effectively through your brand.

Best-known strategies for building a strong brand is creating a memorable logo and tagline. Your logo should be simple, memorable, and reflect your brand's personality. Your tagline should be short and catchy, and communicate what makes you unique. When clients see your logo and tagline, they should immediately think of your brand and what you stand for.

Consistency

One of the best-known strategies for building a strong brand is to create a memorable logo and tagline. Your logo should be distinctive and easy to recognize, while your tagline should be catchy and memorable. This will help you to create a strong visual identity that will stay in the minds of potential clients long after they have interacted with you.

Another important aspect of building a strong brand is consistency. Your brand should be consistent across all platforms, from your website and social media profiles to your business cards and promotional materials. Consistency helps build trust and reinforces your brand's message.

In addition to creating a strong brand, it's important to market yourself effectively both online and offline. In today's digital age, having a strong online presence is essential. Your website should be well-designed, easy to navigate, and optimized for search engines. You should also have a presence on social media platforms like Facebook, Twitter, and LinkedIn, where you can connect with potential clients and share information about your brand.

Offline, there are a variety of strategies you can use to market yourself and build your brand. These include attending networking events, speaking at conferences and seminars, and sponsoring community events. You can also use traditional advertising methods like print ads, direct mail, and billboards.

Having a strong brand is essential for realtors who want to stand out in a crowded market and attract clients. Your brand represents who you are, what you stand for, and what clients can expect when they work with you. To build a strong brand, you need to invest time and effort into understanding your target audience and communicating your unique selling points effectively. Consistency is key, both in your branding and in your marketing efforts both online and offline.

Creating a strong visual identity is crucial to building a successful brand. One of the most effective strategies for building a strong brand is to create a memorable logo and tagline that will set you apart from the competition. Your logo should be distinctive and easy to recognize, while your tagline should be catchy and memorable.

A well-designed logo can instantly communicate your brand's personality and values, while also creating a sense of trust and credibility with potential clients. It should be visually appealing, while also conveying a message that resonates with your target audience. Your logo should be consistent across all of your marketing materials, from your business cards to your website, to help build recognition and familiarity with your brand.

In addition to creating a memorable logo and tagline, it's also important to be consistent in your messaging across all marketing materials. This means using the same font, colors, and design elements across your website, social media profiles, business cards, and other materials. Consistency helps to build trust and familiarity with your brand, which can lead to increased referrals and repeat business.

Your tagline, on the other hand, should be short and sweet, but also powerful enough to leave a lasting impression. It should be memorable and catchy, while also communicating the essence of your brand's message. A great tagline can help set you apart from the competition, while also creating an emotional connection with potential clients.

Investing time and effort into creating a strong visual identity is essential for any real estate agent looking to build a successful brand. It is important to work with a professional designer to create a logo and tagline that accurately reflects your brand's personality and values, and that will resonate with your target audience. By creating a strong visual identity, you can set yourself apart from the competition and build a brand that is memorable, recognizable, and trusted by potential clients.

Consistency is an essential aspect of branding and marketing. Using the same design elements, color scheme, and messaging across all marketing materials creates a consistent and recognizable visual identity that stays in the minds of potential clients long after they have interacted with your brand. This consistency helps to build trust and familiarity, which can lead to increased referrals and repeat business.

Imagine a realtor who uses one logo on their website and business cards, a different logo on their social media profiles, and yet another logo on their marketing flyers. This inconsistency can create confusion among potential clients, making it difficult for them to recognize and remember the realtor's brand. They might wonder if these different logos represent different businesses or if the realtor is not paying enough attention to their brand.

In contrast, a realtor who uses the same logo, font, and color scheme across all marketing materials creates a consistent visual identity that helps potential clients recognize and remember their brand. When clients see this consistency, they feel more confident in the realtor's professionalism and attention to detail, which can make them more likely to choose the realtor for their real estate needs.

Consistency also helps to reinforce your brand messaging. When you use the same messaging and language across all marketing materials, you create a clear and consistent message that potential clients can easily understand and relate to. This consistent message can help to build trust and credibility with your audience, making them more likely to choose you as their realtor.

For example, if you position yourself as an expert in luxury real estate, your messaging should reflect this positioning. You should use language and messaging that speaks to the unique needs and desires of luxury homebuyers, such as highlighting high-end features, exclusive neighborhoods, and top-of-the-line amenities. By consistently using this messaging across all marketing materials, you build a reputation as an expert in luxury real estate, which can attract clients who are specifically looking for that type of expertise.

Consistency is an essential aspect of building a strong brand in real estate. By using the same logo, font, and design elements across all marketing materials, you create a consistent visual identity that helps potential clients recognize and remember your brand. Consistent messaging helps to reinforce your brand positioning and build trust and credibility with your audience. This consistency can ultimately lead to increased referrals and repeat business, making it a vital component of any realtor's marketing strategy

Another important aspect of building a strong brand is to have a clear understanding of your target audience. Who are the clients you want to attract? What are their pain points and what solutions can you offer them? By understanding your audience, you can tailor your messaging and marketing strategies to effectively reach and connect with them.

Understanding your target audience is a crucial aspect of building a strong brand in the real estate industry. Your target audience is the group of people that you want to attract as your clients, and it is essential to have a clear understanding of who they are, what they need, and what they want. By doing so, you can tailor your messaging and marketing strategies to effectively reach and connect with them, increasing the likelihood of generating leads and closing deals.

To identify your target audience, you need to research and analyze their demographics, psychographics, and behaviors. Demographics include age, gender, income, occupation, and location, while psychographics involve understanding their values, attitudes, beliefs, and lifestyles. Behavior, on the other hand, refers to how they interact with your brand and the real estate industry as a whole.

Once you have identified your target audience, you can create messaging and marketing strategies that resonate with them. For instance, if you are targeting first-time homebuyers, you may want to focus on their pain points, such as affordability and the home buying process's complexity. You could create educational materials, such as blog posts or videos, that explain the home buying process in simple terms or offer tips on how to save for a down payment.

By understanding your target audience, you can also determine which marketing channels are most effective in reaching them. For example, if your target audience is millennials, social media platforms such as Instagram or TikTok may be more effective than traditional marketing channels such as print ads or direct mail.

Another crucial aspect of building a strong brand is having a clear and consistent message across all marketing materials. This means using the same font, colors, and design elements across your website, social media profiles, business cards, and other materials. By doing so, you create a strong visual identity that stays in the minds of potential clients long after they have interacted with you.

Consistency in messaging and branding also helps build trust and familiarity with your brand. When clients see a consistent message across different channels, they are more likely to trust your brand and perceive it as reliable and professional. This, in turn, can lead to increased referrals and repeat business.

Understanding your target audience and creating a clear and consistent message are crucial aspects of building a strong brand in the real estate industry. By doing so, you can tailor your messaging and marketing strategies to effectively reach and connect with your target audience, increasing the likelihood of generating leads and closing deals.

Online Marketing

Online marketing is another essential component of building a strong brand in real estate. Your website is your online storefront, and it's important to make a good first impression. Your website should be easy to navigate, visually appealing, and provide valuable information to potential clients. You should also ensure that your website is mobile-friendly, as more and more people are using their smartphones to search for homes and real estate agents.

In today's digital age, online marketing is a crucial element of building a strong brand in real estate. Your website serves as your online storefront, and it is often the first point of contact potential clients have with your brand. Therefore, it is essential to make a good first impression.

One of the most critical aspects of an effective real estate website is ease of navigation. Visitors should be able to find what they are looking for quickly and easily. Your website should have a clear and intuitive layout, with a simple menu structure that allows visitors to navigate to the most relevant information easily.

In addition to being easy to navigate, your website should also be visually appealing. A well-designed website with high-quality images and graphics can help to create a positive impression and encourage visitors to stay longer and explore further. Your website should be consistent with your branding and reflect your personality, values, and mission.

Providing valuable information is another essential element of an effective real estate website. Potential clients should be able to find detailed information about your services, experience, and qualifications. They should also be able to access valuable resources such as market data, neighborhood information, and real estate tips and advice.

Finally, it is important to ensure that your website is mobile-friendly. With more and more people using their smartphones to search for homes and real estate agents, a mobile-responsive website is essential. A mobile-friendly website will provide a positive user experience and help you to connect with potential clients on-the-go.

In addition to your website, social media is another critical component of online marketing for real estate agents. Social media platforms such as Facebook, Instagram, and LinkedIn provide a powerful way to connect with potential clients, build your brand, and showcase your expertise.

Through social media, you can engage with your audience and share valuable content that is relevant and interesting to them. By sharing industry news, market trends, and insights, you can position yourself as a thought leader and build trust and credibility with your followers.

Online marketing is an essential component of building a strong brand in real estate. Your website and social media profiles provide a powerful way to showcase your brand, connect with potential clients, and establish your expertise. By focusing on ease of navigation, visual appeal, valuable information, and mobile-friendliness, you can create a positive first impression and set yourself apart from the competition.

Social media is another powerful tool for building a strong brand and connecting with potential clients. Platforms such as Facebook, Twitter, and Instagram can be used to share your expertise, showcase your listings, and engage with your audience. It's important to post consistently and engage with your followers to build a loyal following.

Social media has become a powerful tool for building a strong brand and connecting with potential clients in the real estate industry. Platforms such as Facebook, Twitter, and Instagram provide real estate agents with the opportunity to showcase their expertise, share their listings, and engage with their audience in a way that was never possible before.

One of the key benefits of using social media for real estate marketing is the ability to reach a wider audience. With over 3 billion active social media users worldwide, these platforms provide an excellent opportunity to connect with potential clients who may not have otherwise heard about you or your business. By posting regularly and engaging with your followers, you can build a loyal following that is interested in your expertise and services.

Another advantage of social media is the ability to showcase your expertise in a particular area of real estate. Whether you specialize in luxury properties or first-time homebuyers, social media provides a platform to share your knowledge and provide valuable insights to your audience. This can help establish you as a trusted expert in your field, which can lead to increased referrals and repeat business.

To make the most out of your social media efforts, it's important to post consistently and engage with your followers. Consistency is key when it comes to building a strong brand, as it helps to reinforce your messaging and establish your presence on these platforms. Posting regular updates about your listings, sharing valuable insights about the real estate market, and engaging with your audience can help keep your followers engaged and interested in your brand.

Engaging with your followers is also crucial when it comes to building a loyal following on social media. Responding to comments and messages in a timely manner, sharing user-generated content, and running contests or giveaways are all great ways to connect with your audience and build a sense of community around your brand.

When it comes to using social media for real estate marketing, it's important to choose the right platforms for your business. While Facebook and Instagram are popular choices for real estate agents, platforms such as LinkedIn and Twitter can also be effective for reaching a professional audience or providing timely updates about the market.

In addition to social media, email marketing can also be a powerful tool for building a strong brand and connecting with potential clients. By sending regular newsletters and updates to your email list, you can keep your audience informed about your business and provide valuable insights about the real estate market.

Overall, building a strong brand in real estate requires a multi-faceted approach that includes a combination of online and offline marketing strategies. By investing time and effort into building a strong brand, real estate agents can attract more clients, establish themselves as experts in their field, and ultimately increase their business and revenue

Offline marketing strategies are also important for building a strong brand. Networking events, community involvement, and sponsoring local events can help you to build relationships and establish yourself as a trusted authority in your community. Additionally, print materials such as brochures, flyers, and postcards can be used to promote your services and increase your visibility.

While online marketing is an important aspect of building a strong brand in real estate, offline marketing strategies are just as crucial. In fact, offline marketing can often be more effective at building relationships and establishing trust with potential clients. There are several offline marketing strategies that real estate agents can use to build a strong brand and increase their visibility in their community.

One effective offline marketing strategy is networking events. Attending networking events, such as business luncheons, industry conferences, and local meetups, allows real estate agents to connect with other professionals in their industry and build relationships with potential clients. By attending these events, real estate agents can establish themselves as trusted authorities in their field and increase their visibility in their community.

Community involvement is another effective offline marketing strategy. By participating in local events, such as charity fundraisers, community clean-up events, and school fundraisers, real estate agents can show their support for their community and establish themselves as community leaders. This can help to build trust with potential clients and increase their visibility in their community.

Sponsoring local events is another way to increase visibility and build relationships in your community. Real estate agents can sponsor local events, such as charity walks, little league games, or community concerts, by donating money or resources. This not only helps to support the community but also helps to build brand recognition and establish the agent as a trusted authority in the area.

Print materials such as brochures, flyers, and postcards can also be used to promote a real estate agent's services and increase visibility. These materials can be distributed at networking events, community events, and even mailed directly to potential clients. It is important to design these materials carefully, using the same brand elements and messaging as your website and other marketing materials, to create a cohesive brand identity.

In conclusion, while online marketing is an essential component of building a strong brand in real estate, offline marketing strategies are equally important. By attending networking events, participating in community events, sponsoring local events, and using print materials, real estate agents can increase their visibility, build relationships, and establish themselves as trusted authorities in their community.

Building a strong brand is essential for success in the real estate industry. Creating a memorable logo and tagline, being consistent in your messaging, understanding your target audience, and utilizing online and offline marketing strategies are all important components of a successful branding strategy. By investing time and effort into building a strong brand, you can attract new clients, generate referrals, and ultimately achieve long-term success in the industry.

CHAPTER 3: DEVELOPING EXPERTISE

As a real estate agent, one of the most important things you can do to succeed in the industry is to develop expertise in a particular niche or market. This means focusing on a specific type of property or client, and becoming an expert in that area. While it may seem counterintuitive to limit your potential client pool, specializing in a particular niche can actually bring many benefits to your business.

When it comes to developing expertise in a particular niche or market, some real estate agents might worry that narrowing their focus will limit their potential client pool. However, this is not necessarily the case, and in fact, limiting your pool of potential clients can be beneficial in many ways.

First and foremost, when you specialize in a particular area, you become an expert in that field. This expertise sets you apart from other agents who may not have the same level of knowledge or experience. When potential clients are looking for a real estate agent to work with, they often look for someone who has specific knowledge and experience in their particular situation or needs. By specializing in a niche, you can position yourself as the go-to expert for those clients.

Another advantage of specializing is that you can streamline your marketing efforts. Instead of trying to appeal to a broad range of clients, you can focus your marketing efforts on a specific target audience. This can save you time, money, and effort, as you can tailor your messaging and marketing strategies to more effectively reach and connect with your ideal clients.

Moreover, by limiting your potential client pool, you can also create a sense of exclusivity around your brand. If you specialize in luxury homes, for example, clients may feel that working with you is a privilege and that they are receiving a higher level of service and attention than they might receive from a generalist agent. This exclusivity can make clients more willing to pay a premium for your services and can help to build your reputation in the industry.

It's also important to note that while you may be limiting your potential client pool, you are not necessarily limiting your income. When you specialize in a particular niche, you can often charge higher fees for your services, as you are providing a higher level of expertise and service. Additionally, by becoming an expert in your field, you may be able to tap into a higher-priced market that you may not have had access to as a generalist.

While it may seem counterintuitive to limit your potential client pool, specializing in a particular niche or market can be incredibly beneficial for your real estate business. It allows you to position yourself as an expert, streamline your marketing efforts, create a sense of exclusivity around your brand, and potentially charge higher fees for your services. By taking the time to develop your expertise and focus on a specific area of the industry, you can set yourself apart from the competition and build a successful and sustainable real estate business.

By focusing on a particular niche or market, you can actually improve the quality of your client base, as well as increase your success rate. When you specialize in a particular area, you become an expert in that field, which means that you can provide your clients with a level of knowledge and insight that they may not be able to find elsewhere.

Additionally, by limiting your potential client pool, you can actually increase your chances of success. When you specialize, you can target a specific group of people and tailor your marketing efforts towards them. This means that you can focus on building relationships with these individuals and establishing yourself as a trusted authority in your field.

For example, if you specialize in luxury homes, you can focus your marketing efforts on individuals who are looking to buy or sell high-end properties. You can attend exclusive networking events, advertise in luxury publications, and build relationships with high-net-worth individuals. By doing so, you can position yourself as an expert in the luxury home market, which can lead to more business and higher commissions.

In addition, when you limit your potential client pool, you can also increase your efficiency and effectiveness. When you have a clear understanding of your target audience, you can tailor your messaging and marketing efforts towards them, which can save you time and resources. You can also focus your efforts on building relationships with these individuals, which can lead to more referrals and repeat business.

Overall, specializing in a particular niche or market is not counterintuitive, but rather a strategic approach to building a successful real estate business. By becoming an expert in a particular field, you can provide your clients with a level of knowledge and insight that they may not be able to find elsewhere. Additionally, by limiting your potential client pool, you can increase your chances of success, efficiency, and effectiveness.

Firstly, specializing in a niche allows you to become an expert in that area. By dedicating your time and energy to understanding the intricacies of a particular market or type of property, you can provide your clients with a level of knowledge and expertise that generalist agents cannot match. This can lead to higher client satisfaction, as your clients will appreciate your ability to provide them with valuable insights and advice.

Furthermore, being a specialist in a particular niche can help you to stand out in a crowded market. In today's world, there are many real estate agents out there, and it can be difficult to differentiate yourself from the competition. However, by focusing on a specific niche, you can establish yourself as an expert in that area, and attract clients who are looking for someone with your particular expertise. This can lead to increased visibility and referrals, as clients who are looking for a specialist in your niche are more likely to recommend you to others.

Another benefit of specializing in a niche is that it allows you to tailor your marketing efforts to a specific audience. By understanding the needs and wants of your target market, you can create marketing materials that speak directly to them. This can help to increase the effectiveness of your marketing campaigns, as you are able to connect with potential clients on a deeper level.

In addition, specializing in a niche can help to simplify your business operations. By focusing on a specific area, you can streamline your processes and become more efficient in your work. This can lead to increased productivity, as you are able to complete tasks more quickly and effectively.

There are many different niches that you can specialize in as a real estate agent, depending on your interests and expertise. Some examples include luxury properties, vacation homes, first-time homebuyers, and seniors. By choosing a niche that resonates with you and your skills, you can set yourself up for success in the industry.

Overall, developing expertise in a particular niche or market can bring many benefits to your real estate business. From increased client satisfaction to improved marketing efforts and more streamlined operations, specializing in a niche can help you to stand out in a crowded market and establish yourself as a trusted expert in your field.

Expertise

Developing expertise in a particular area of real estate can be a powerful way to differentiate yourself from other agents and build a reputation as a go-to expert in your field. Whether you're interested in luxury homes, first-time buyers, probate sales, or another niche field, there are a few key steps you can take to develop your expertise and build your reputation.

The first step is to research and study the particular area of real estate you're interested in. This might involve reading industry publications, attending workshops or seminars, and even taking specialized courses. By immersing yourself in the subject matter, you can gain a deeper understanding of the market, the needs of clients in that market, and the best practices for serving them.

The next step is to gain practical experience in your chosen area of expertise. This might involve taking on clients in that area, even if they're not paying top dollar, in order to build up your skills and knowledge. By working with real clients, you can learn the nuances of the market, build your network, and develop your own unique approach to serving clients in that area.

Another way to develop expertise in a particular area is to seek out mentorship or guidance from more experienced agents in that field. This might involve reaching out to other agents in your area who specialize in the same niche, attending industry events, or joining online communities where you can connect with other agents and learn from their experiences.

Seeking out mentorship can be a powerful way to accelerate your growth and development as a real estate professional. A mentor is someone who has been in the industry for a long time and has gained a wealth of knowledge and experience that they can share with you. Mentors can offer insights and guidance that you might not get elsewhere, and they can help you avoid common pitfalls that can hold you back.

Finding a mentor can seem daunting at first, but there are many ways to go about it. One of the best ways is to simply ask around. Reach out to other real estate professionals that you know or admire and see if they would be willing to mentor you. You might be surprised at how willing people are to help out, especially if they see potential in you.

Another way to find a mentor is to attend industry events and conferences. These events are often attended by successful real estate professionals who are eager to share their knowledge and connect with others in the industry. Attend workshops, sessions, and networking events and look for opportunities to connect with people who could be potential mentors.

Online communities can also be a great source of mentorship. Joining Facebook groups, LinkedIn groups, or other online forums for real estate professionals can connect you with people who are experts in your niche or market. You can ask questions, share your experiences, and learn from the wisdom of others.

Once you have found a potential mentor, it's important to approach them in the right way. Be respectful of their time and their expertise, and be clear about what you hope to gain from the relationship. Listen to their advice and guidance, and be willing to put in the work to apply what you learn.

Remember that mentorship is a two-way street. While you can benefit from the guidance and expertise of your mentor, they can also benefit from your enthusiasm and fresh perspective. Be open to the possibility of building a long-lasting relationship with your mentor, and be sure to express your gratitude for their time and insights. With the right mentor by your side, you can accelerate your growth as a real estate professional and achieve your goals more quickly than you ever thought possible.

Another way to seek out mentorship is to attend industry events and conferences. These events are great opportunities to network with other professionals in your field and to learn from their experiences. Look for events that focus on your area of specialization or that feature speakers who are experts in that area. Attend their sessions and take notes on their insights and advice. After the event, try to connect with them on social media or email to establish a relationship and ask any further questions you may have.

You can also consider joining professional organizations or associations that are specific to your niche. These organizations provide a community of like-minded professionals who can offer support, advice, and mentorship. Attend their meetings, participate in their online forums, and take advantage of any other resources they offer. Some organizations even have mentorship programs where they pair up experienced members with newer members.

Finally, don't be afraid to reach out to professionals in your area of expertise directly. Send a friendly email introducing yourself and asking if they would be willing to meet for coffee or a phone call to discuss your career goals and get their advice. Many professionals are happy to help and may even be flattered by your interest in their work.

In conclusion, seeking out mentorship is a great way to develop your expertise and grow your career. Look for opportunities to learn from experienced professionals, whether it be through formal mentorship programs, networking events, or reaching out directly. By seeking out mentorship, you can gain valuable insights and guidance to help you navigate your career path and achieve your goals.

Networking is also crucial when developing expertise in a particular area. Attend industry events, join local real estate organizations, and participate in community events. Being an active part of your local community will help you to build your reputation as a trusted expert in your field.

Finally, don't be afraid to market yourself as an expert in your chosen niche. Create targeted marketing materials that showcase your expertise, such as brochures or website content that highlights your knowledge and experience in your chosen area of real estate. By promoting yourself as an expert in your niche, you can attract clients who are specifically looking for an agent with your skills and knowledge.

Marketing yourself as an expert in your chosen niche is one of the most effective ways to build expertise and become a go-to professional in your field. By narrowing your focus and becoming an expert in a particular niche, you can establish yourself as a specialist in your industry, differentiate yourself from other agents, and attract clients who are specifically looking for your unique set of skills.

To begin marketing yourself as an expert, the first step is to choose a niche. This could be anything from luxury homes, to first-time buyers, to probate or seller-only properties. Once you've chosen your niche, it's important to develop a deep understanding of the market, including the specific needs and pain points of your target audience.

Next, you can begin to tailor your marketing efforts to your chosen niche. This may involve creating content that speaks directly to the needs and interests of your target audience, such as blog posts, social media posts, or email newsletters. You may also want to attend networking events and conferences that are specific to your niche, and join online forums or groups where you can connect with others in your industry.

Another effective way to market yourself as an expert in your niche is to showcase your expertise through your website and other marketing materials. This may involve creating a section on your website that is dedicated to your niche, featuring testimonials from satisfied clients, and highlighting your relevant experience and qualifications.

Ultimately, the goal of marketing yourself as an expert in your niche is to establish yourself as a trusted authority in your industry. By focusing your efforts on a specific niche, you can position yourself as a specialist and differentiate yourself from other agents in your area. Over time, as you build your expertise and establish your reputation, you may find that clients seek you out specifically for your unique skills and expertise, helping to further grow your business and solidify your position as a top professional in your field.

Once you have identified your niche and developed your expertise, it's important to start marketing yourself as an expert in your chosen field. Here are some steps to take to market yourself effectively:

1. Create a professional brand: Your brand should communicate your expertise and specialization. This means creating a logo and tagline that communicate what you do, and a consistent visual identity that is reflected across all of your marketing materials. This will help you stand out in a crowded market and establish yourself as a professional.

2. Build a strong online presence: In today's digital age, having a strong online presence is essential. Start by creating a professional website that showcases your expertise and services. Make sure your website is easy to navigate, visually

appealing, and provides valuable information to potential clients. You can also use social media platforms like Facebook, Twitter, and LinkedIn to share your expertise and engage with potential clients.

3. Focus on content marketing: Content marketing is a powerful way to establish yourself as an expert in your niche. This means creating and sharing valuable content that is relevant to your target audience. For example, if you specialize in luxury homes, you could write blog posts about luxury home design trends, showcase luxury homes on your website and social media platforms, and create videos or webinars that educate potential clients about the luxury home market.

4. Attend industry events: Industry events such as conferences and seminars are a great way to network with other professionals in your field and stay up-to-date on industry trends and changes. Attend events that are relevant to your niche and be sure to connect with other attendees and speakers.

5. Leverage client testimonials: Client testimonials are a powerful way to demonstrate your expertise and the value you provide to your clients. Ask satisfied clients to provide testimonials and share them on your website, social media platforms, and other marketing materials.

By following these steps and consistently marketing yourself as an expert in your chosen niche, you can establish yourself as a trusted authority and attract more clients who are seeking your specialized services.

Developing expertise in a particular area of real estate can be a powerful way to differentiate yourself from other agents and build a reputation as a go-to expert in your field. By studying, gaining practical experience, seeking mentorship, networking, and promoting yourself as an expert, you can establish yourself as a trusted authority in your niche and attract clients who are specifically looking for an agent with your skills and knowledge.

Always Stay Up-To-Date

Staying up-to-date on industry trends and changes is essential for real estate agents who want to maintain a competitive edge and provide the best service possible to their clients. The real estate industry is constantly evolving, with new technology, market shifts, and regulations affecting the way agents do business. To remain relevant and knowledgeable, agents must make a conscious effort to stay informed and educated on the latest trends and changes in their field.

One of the best strategies for staying up-to-date on industry trends and changes is to attend industry conferences and events. These events provide opportunities for agents to learn from industry leaders and experts, network with peers, and gain insight into emerging trends and technologies. Conferences and events can also offer continuing education credits, which are often required for agents to maintain their licenses.

In addition to attending conferences and events, real estate agents can stay up-to-date by reading industry publications and blogs. There are many publications and blogs that cover the real estate industry, including national and local news outlets, trade publications, and individual agent blogs. By regularly reading these sources, agents can gain valuable insights into industry trends, market shifts, and best practices.

Another way to stay informed is to join industry associations and groups. These organizations offer opportunities for agents to connect with peers, share knowledge and best practices, and gain access to resources and educational materials. Associations also often provide updates on industry trends and changes, as well as advocacy efforts on behalf of the industry.

Real estate agents can stay up-to-date by working with mentors or coaches who have extensive experience and knowledge in their field. Mentors and coaches can provide guidance, advice, and support, as well as share their own experiences and insights. Working with a mentor or coach can be especially beneficial for agents who are just starting out in the industry or who are looking to specialize in a particular niche.

Staying up-to-date on industry trends and changes is essential for real estate agents who want to succeed in their field. By attending conferences and events, reading industry publications and blogs, joining industry associations and groups, and working with mentors or coaches, agents can develop the knowledge and expertise they need to provide the best service possible to their clients.

Continuing on the topic of staying up-to-date on industry trends and changes, one of the most effective strategies is attending industry conferences and events. These events provide the opportunity to learn from experts in the field, network with other professionals, and stay informed on the latest industry developments. It's important to attend conferences and events related to your niche area, as well as broader real estate events that cover a range of topics.

Another way to stay up-to-date is by reading industry publications, such as real estate journals, blogs, and newsletters. These publications often provide insights into the latest industry trends and changes, as well as practical advice for real estate professionals. It's important to stay informed on both local and national trends, as they can impact your niche area and overall business strategy.

In addition to attending events and reading industry publications, it's also important to stay connected with other professionals in your field. This can be done through joining industry associations, such as the National Association of Realtors, as well as local real estate organizations. These associations provide opportunities for networking, as well as access to educational resources and industry news.

Another strategy for staying up-to-date is by using technology to your advantage. There are a variety of apps and online tools that can help you stay organized, manage your clients and transactions, and stay informed on industry news and trends. It's important to explore different tools and platforms and find ones that work best for your business and niche area.

Finally, it's important to never stop learning and growing. Continuing education courses and certifications can help you develop new skills and stay up-to-date on industry changes. It's also important to seek feedback from clients and colleagues, and continuously evaluate and improve your business strategy.

Continuing education is an essential aspect of developing and maintaining expertise in any field, and real estate is no exception. Even after obtaining a license and completing the required coursework, there is still much to learn about the industry and its ever-changing landscape. As a real estate professional, it's crucial to stay up-to-date on market trends, industry regulations, and new technologies to better serve clients and maintain a competitive edge.

One way to pursue continuing education in real estate is by attending industry conferences, workshops, and seminars. These events offer opportunities to network with other professionals and learn from industry experts who share their insights and knowledge. They also provide valuable continuing education credits that can be used to fulfill licensing requirements.

Another way to pursue continuing education is through online courses and webinars. There are many online resources available, including webinars hosted by industry leaders, professional organizations, and real estate companies. These courses can be accessed from anywhere, making them a convenient option for busy professionals.

Real estate agents can also seek out mentorship opportunities to gain new insights and perspectives from experienced professionals. This can involve seeking guidance from a more experienced colleague or even hiring a coach or consultant to provide specialized training and support.

Furthermore, reading industry publications, such as real estate magazines and newsletters, can help professionals stay informed about industry news, trends, and best practices. Joining professional organizations and networking groups is also an effective way to stay connected with other professionals in the industry and gain access to valuable resources and information.

In addition to staying informed, pursuing continuing education demonstrates a commitment to professionalism and ongoing growth.

It also positions real estate professionals as experts in their field, which can lead to increased credibility and opportunities for referrals and repeat business.

Overall, continuing education is an essential component of developing and maintaining expertise in real estate. Whether through conferences, online courses, mentorship, or reading industry publications, professionals can stay informed and up-to-date on industry trends and best practices, leading to greater success in the industry.

Staying up-to-date on industry trends and changes is essential for developing expertise and staying competitive in the real estate industry. Attending conferences and events, reading industry publications, staying connected with other professionals, using technology, and continuing education are all effective strategies for staying informed and growing your business.

Developing expertise in any field, including real estate, not only benefits you financially but also plays a crucial role in providing top-notch client service. When you become an expert in your chosen area, you become a trusted advisor and resource for your clients, guiding them through the complexities of the real estate process and helping them achieve their goals. Let's delve into the various ways in which developing expertise benefits you and your clients.

Financial Benefits:

1. Increased Market Value: By specializing and developing expertise in a specific niche, you position yourself as an authority in that area. Clients are often willing to pay a premium for the expertise and specialized knowledge you bring to the table, allowing you to command higher commissions and fees.
2. Competitive Advantage: Developing expertise sets you apart from the competition. When clients perceive you as an expert in a particular market or field, they are more likely to choose you over other agents who lack the same level of knowledge

and experience. This competitive advantage can lead to a higher volume of transactions and greater financial success.

3. Referrals and Repeat Business: Clients are more likely to refer their friends, family, and colleagues to an agent who has demonstrated expertise and provided exceptional service. Word-of-mouth referrals are a powerful source of business, and by becoming an expert, you increase the likelihood of receiving referrals from satisfied clients. Additionally, when you deliver exceptional service and demonstrate your expertise, clients are more likely to work with you again in the future, generating repeat business and a steady stream of income.

Benefits to Clients:

1. Specialized Knowledge: By developing expertise in a specific niche, you gain a deep understanding of the market dynamics, trends, and challenges associated with that niche. This specialized knowledge allows you to provide clients with accurate and valuable insights, helping them make informed decisions. Clients benefit from your expertise by receiving tailored advice and solutions that cater to their unique needs and goals.

2. Streamlined Process: When you are well-versed in your area of expertise, you can guide clients through the real estate process with confidence and efficiency. You anticipate challenges, offer proactive solutions, and navigate complex situations with ease, ensuring a smooth and seamless experience for your clients. This level of expertise saves clients time, reduces stress, and increases their overall satisfaction.

3. Access to Networks and Resources: Developing expertise often involves building strong connections and networks within your chosen niche. This means that you can provide clients with access to a wide range of resources, including trusted professionals such as lenders, inspectors, contractors,

and other industry experts. This network of trusted partners enhances the client experience and adds value to your service.

Ultimately, developing expertise not only benefits you financially but also greatly benefits your clients by providing them with top-tier service, specialized knowledge, and a seamless real estate experience. By continuously expanding your knowledge, staying current with market trends, and honing your skills, you position yourself as a valuable resource and trusted advisor in your field. This dedication to expertise leads to long-lasting client relationships, referrals, and a thriving real estate business.

In addition to the financial benefits and enhanced client service, developing expertise in your field brings further advantages to both you and your clients.

1. Problem Solving and Mitigating Risks: As an expert, you possess a deep understanding of the intricacies and potential pitfalls within your niche. This allows you to identify and address potential issues before they arise, minimizing risks for your clients. Your expertise enables you to navigate complex transactions, negotiate effectively on their behalf, and find creative solutions to challenges that may arise during the buying or selling process. By mitigating risks and resolving problems efficiently, you instill confidence in your clients and establish yourself as a reliable and knowledgeable professional.

2. Market Insights and Analysis: By specializing in a particular niche, you develop a keen sense of the market dynamics, trends, and patterns specific to that area. This expertise empowers you to provide clients with accurate and up-to-date market insights, enabling them to make informed decisions. Whether it's pricing their property competitively, identifying lucrative investment opportunities, or understanding market fluctuations, your expertise equips clients with valuable information that supports their real estate goals.

3. Trust and Reputation Building: Developing expertise enhances your credibility and builds a strong reputation within your

industry and community. Clients seek out professionals who are knowledgeable, trustworthy, and have a proven track record of success. By positioning yourself as an expert, you gain the trust and respect of your clients, colleagues, and other industry professionals. This trust translates into increased referrals, positive reviews, and a strong professional network, further solidifying your reputation as a go-to real estate expert.

4. Innovation and Adaptability: As you delve deeper into your chosen niche, you naturally become more attuned to emerging trends, technologies, and best practices within that field. This knowledge allows you to stay ahead of the curve and embrace innovation, offering your clients cutting-edge solutions and a competitive advantage. By continuously adapting to the evolving landscape of real estate, you demonstrate your commitment to providing exceptional service and remaining at the forefront of your industry.

5. Personal Fulfillment and Growth: Developing expertise in your field is a fulfilling and personally rewarding journey. It allows you to delve into a subject you are passionate about, continually expand your knowledge, and become a lifelong learner. The pursuit of expertise keeps you engaged, motivated, and excited about your profession, ultimately benefiting both you and your clients.

By focusing on developing expertise in your chosen niche, you establish yourself as a trusted authority, set yourself apart from the competition, and attract clients who value your specialized knowledge and skills. It is a strategic investment in your professional growth, financial success, and the overall satisfaction of your clients. As you continue to hone your expertise, remember to communicate your knowledge effectively, stay updated on industry trends, and consistently deliver exceptional service. Your dedication to expertise will be the foundation of a thriving real estate career and a source of immense value for your clients.

CHAPTER 4: PROVIDING EXCEPTIONAL CUSTOMER SERVICE

In the world of real estate, providing exceptional customer service is not just a buzzword; it is a fundamental aspect of building a successful and enduring career. Going above and beyond to exceed your clients' expectations, being responsive and communicative, and prioritizing their needs and concerns are all key ingredients to providing exceptional customer service. In this chapter, we will explore in vivid detail the importance of providing exceptional customer service, how it positively impacts your overall business and personal life, and step-by-step strategies to deliver an outstanding experience to your clients.

The Importance of Exceptional Customer Service

Building Trust and Loyalty:

Exceptional customer service is the cornerstone of building trust and fostering long-term client relationships. By consistently delivering exceptional service, you create a positive experience that clients will remember and want to repeat. When clients trust you and feel valued, they are more likely to refer you to friends and family, provide positive testimonials, and become repeat customers themselves. This not only leads to a steady stream of referrals and repeat business but also contributes to your reputation as a trusted and reliable realtor in the community.

Setting Yourself Apart:
In a competitive real estate market, providing exceptional customer service sets you apart from your competitors. It becomes your unique selling proposition and a key differentiator that attracts clients to choose you over others. When clients experience exceptional service, they are more likely to remember you, recommend you, and seek your services again in the future. Your commitment to going above and beyond demonstrates professionalism, expertise, and a genuine dedication to meeting their needs.

The Positive Impact on Your Business

Increased Referrals:
Providing exceptional customer service creates a ripple effect of positive word-of-mouth advertising. Satisfied clients become your brand ambassadors, eagerly referring their friends, family, and colleagues to your services. This leads to a steady flow of referrals, expanding your client base and generating new business opportunities. By consistently delivering exceptional service, you cultivate a reputation as the go-to realtor in your area, resulting in a continuous stream of referrals that can sustain and grow your business over time.

Repeat Business:
Exceptional customer service is the catalyst for repeat business. When clients have a positive experience with you, they are more likely to turn to you for their future real estate needs. Repeat business not only reduces your reliance on constantly finding new clients but also saves you time and effort in building new relationships from scratch. By nurturing your existing client base through exceptional service, you cultivate long-term client loyalty and become their trusted advisor in all their real estate endeavors.

The Positive Impact on Your Personal Life

Professional Fulfillment:
Providing exceptional customer service goes beyond financial success. It brings a sense of professional fulfillment and satisfaction that comes from knowing you have made a positive impact on your clients' lives. When you genuinely care about your clients' needs and go the extra mile to meet and exceed their expectations, it brings a deep sense of fulfillment and purpose to your work. The knowledge that you have helped clients achieve their real estate goals and created a positive experience for them contributes to your own personal and professional growth.

Personal Relationships and Reputation:
Exceptional customer service extends beyond the transactional aspect of real estate. It fosters meaningful connections and builds long-lasting relationships with clients. By providing exceptional service, you become more than just a realtor; you become a trusted confidant and advisor. These strong relationships not only enhance your business but also enrich your personal life. As clients become friends, you build a network of satisfied clients who appreciate your integrity, expertise, and dedication to their well-being. This reputation as a reliable and caring professional extends beyond the confines of your
business and positively impacts your personal life as well.

Providing exceptional customer service is not just a business strategy; it is a way of life. By prioritizing your clients' needs, going above and beyond their expectations, and consistently delivering outstanding service, you create a positive and memorable experience that sets you apart from your competitors. The impact of exceptional customer service on your business and personal life is far-reaching, leading to increased referrals, repeat business, professional fulfillment, and meaningful relationships. Embracing the mindset of providing exceptional customer service is not only essential for the successful longevity of a realtor but also contributes to a fulfilling and rewarding career and personal life.

Strategies for Providing Exceptional Customer Service

Active Listening:

One of the most important aspects of providing exceptional customer service is active listening. Take the time to truly understand your clients' needs, concerns, and preferences. Show genuine empathy and be present in every interaction. By actively listening, you demonstrate that their satisfaction and well-being are your top priorities. This allows you to tailor your services to their specific requirements and create a personalized experience that exceeds their expectations.

Effective Communication:

Clear and timely communication is crucial in providing exceptional customer service. Be responsive to your clients' inquiries, whether it's through phone calls, emails, or text messages. Keep them informed throughout the entire buying or selling process, providing updates and addressing any questions or concerns they may have. By maintaining open lines of communication, you instill confidence and trust in your clients, making them feel valued and reassured.

Attention to Detail:

Paying attention to the smallest details can make a significant difference in providing exceptional customer service. Remember important dates, preferences, and specific requirements that your clients have shared with you. Take note of their preferences for property features, neighborhoods, or amenities. By demonstrating your attention to detail, you show that you genuinely care about their individual needs and are committed to finding the perfect property or achieving the best outcome for them.

Going Above and Beyond:

Exceptional customer service often involves going the extra mile for your clients. Look for opportunities to exceed their expectations and surprise them with added value. This could involve arranging personalized property tours, providing them with comprehensive market analysis reports, or connecting them with trusted professionals in related industries. By going above and beyond, you create a memorable experience that leaves a lasting impression on your clients.

Continuous Improvement:

To consistently provide exceptional customer service, it's essential to embrace a mindset of continuous improvement. Seek feedback from your clients and actively listen to their suggestions. Analyze your interactions and transactions to identify areas where you can enhance your service delivery. Stay updated on industry trends, technologies, and best practices through professional development and education. By constantly striving to improve, you demonstrate your commitment to providing the best possible experience for your clients.

Providing exceptional customer service is a cornerstone of success in the real estate industry. It not only sets you apart from your competitors but also creates long-lasting relationships with your clients. By actively listening, effectively communicating, paying attention to detail, going above and beyond, and embracing continuous improvement, you can consistently deliver outstanding service that exceeds your clients' expectations. Remember, exceptional customer service is not just about completing transactions; it's about creating positive experiences, building trust, and establishing yourself as a trusted advisor in the industry. By prioritizing exceptional customer service, you ensure the successful longevity of your real estate career and positively impact the lives of your clients.

Fostering Effective Communication:

Active listening is a key component of effective communication. When you listen attentively to your clients, you are better able to understand their perspective, gather relevant information, and communicate your ideas and recommendations in a way that resonates with them. By fostering effective communication through active listening, you can avoid misunderstandings, clarify any uncertainties, and ensure that you and your clients are on the same page throughout the real estate process. This promotes transparency and minimizes the chances of miscommunication, leading to smoother transactions and happier clients.

Anticipating and Exceeding Expectations:

By actively listening to your clients' needs and concerns, you can go beyond meeting their expectations and strive to exceed them. Listening allows you to uncover their unspoken desires and preferences, enabling you to anticipate their needs and proactively address any potential issues. This level of attentiveness and proactive approach demonstrates your commitment to providing exceptional service. When you consistently exceed expectations, you not only delight your clients but also cultivate strong word-of-mouth referrals and repeat business, as they become advocates for your services.

Enhancing Client Satisfaction and Loyalty:
Listening is a fundamental aspect of delivering a positive client experience. When you actively listen and address your clients' needs and concerns, you enhance their overall satisfaction with your services. Satisfied clients are more likely to become loyal clients who return for future transactions and refer you to their friends, family, and colleagues. By prioritizing listening as a core part of your customer service strategy, you build long-lasting relationships with clients who trust and value your expertise. This ultimately contributes to your business's success and helps you establish a solid reputation in the real estate industry.

Continuous Improvement and Growth:
Listening to your clients' needs and concerns provides you with valuable feedback that you can use to continuously improve and grow as a real estate professional. By actively listening and seeking feedback from your clients, you gain insights into areas where you can enhance your service, refine your processes, or acquire additional knowledge and skills. This commitment to continuous improvement positions you as a proactive and dedicated agent who is always striving to deliver the best possible outcomes for your clients. As you evolve and grow, you become an even more valuable resource to your clients, attracting new business and generating referrals.

Listening to your clients' needs and concerns is not only important but essential in providing exceptional customer service as a real estate professional. By actively listening, you foster effective communication, anticipate and exceed expectations, enhance client satisfaction and loyalty, and facilitate continuous improvement and growth. When you prioritize listening, you create a client-centered approach that builds trust, cultivates strong relationships, and sets you apart from your competitors. By consistently delivering exceptional customer service through active listening, you establish yourself as a trusted advisor in the real estate industry and position yourself for long-term success.

Providing Exceptional Customer Service Throughout the Buying or Selling Process

Setting the Foundation for Outstanding Customer Service

1. Establish a Positive First Impression: Begin by greeting your clients warmly, whether it's in person, over the phone, or through email. Make them feel welcomed and valued from the very beginning.
2. Build Rapport and Trust: Take the time to get to know your clients on a personal level. Show genuine interest in their goals, preferences, and concerns. By building a strong rapport, you establish a foundation of trust and open communication.

Clear and Transparent Communication

1. Be Responsive and Timely: Respond to your clients' inquiries and requests promptly. Keep them informed of any updates, progress, or changes throughout the buying or selling process. Being proactive in your communication shows that you value their time and are committed to keeping them well-informed.
2. Use Clear and Simple Language: Avoid using jargon or complex terminology that may confuse your clients. Explain concepts and processes in a way that is easy for them to understand. This ensures effective communication and helps them feel more confident and informed.

Going Above and Beyond

1. Personalize the Experience: Tailor your approach to meet the specific needs and preferences of each client. Pay attention to their unique circumstances and offer personalized solutions or

recommendations. This level of personalization demonstrates your commitment to going above and beyond.
2. Provide Proactive Guidance: Anticipate your clients' needs and offer proactive guidance throughout the buying or selling process. Share relevant market insights, provide resources, and offer advice to help them make informed decisions. This proactive approach shows that you are dedicated to their success and well-being.

Attention to Detail

1. Pay Close Attention to Client Preferences: Take note of your clients' preferences for property features, location, budget, and any other relevant factors. Keep a record of these details and use them to refine your search or marketing efforts. This attention to detail demonstrates your commitment to finding the best-fit solutions for your clients.
2. Organize and Streamline Processes: Ensure that your administrative processes are efficient and well-organized. Keep track of important documents, deadlines, and appointments to avoid any unnecessary delays or confusion. A well-structured and streamlined process enhances the overall customer experience.

Problem-Solving and Conflict Resolution

1. Act as a Problem-Solver: Real estate transactions can encounter challenges along the way. Approach problems as opportunities to find solutions. Be proactive in addressing any issues that arise, seeking win-win resolutions for all parties involved.
2. Remain Calm and Professional: In situations where conflicts or disagreements arise, maintain a calm and professional demeanor. Listen attentively to all parties involved and work towards finding a resolution that satisfies everyone. Your ability to handle conflicts gracefully will further enhance your reputation and build trust.

Post-Transaction Follow-Up

1. Express Gratitude and Appreciation: After completing a transaction, take the time to thank your clients for choosing to work with you. Show your appreciation for their trust and support throughout the process. A genuine expression of gratitude reinforces the positive experience they had working with you.
2. Seek Feedback: Request feedback from your clients to gain insights into their experience. This feedback can help you identify areas of improvement and further refine your customer service approach. Additionally, it provides an opportunity to address any remaining concerns and ensure their satisfaction.

Providing outstanding customer service throughout the buying or selling process is crucial for building lasting relationships, generating referrals, and establishing a stellar reputation in the real estate industry. By setting a positive foundation, communicating clearly and transparently, going above and beyond, paying attention to detail, and resolving conflicts effectively, you create an exceptional customer experience. By following these step-by-step guidelines, you can ensure that your clients receive the highest level of service and support, leading to their satisfaction, repeat business, and enthusiastic referrals.

Continuous Improvement

1. Embrace a Growth Mindset: Recognize that providing exceptional customer service is an ongoing process of growth and improvement. Stay open to feedback, both positive and constructive, and use it as an opportunity to learn and develop your skills further.
2. Seek Professional Development Opportunities: Invest in your own professional development by attending workshops, seminars, or industry conferences. These events provide valuable insights, updates on industry trends, and networking opportunities to enhance your knowledge and skills.
3. Stay Informed: Stay up-to-date with industry news, market trends, and changes in regulations or laws that may impact

your clients. Regularly read industry publications, follow reputable real estate blogs, and engage in discussions with colleagues to stay informed and knowledgeable.

4. Learn from Experienced Professionals: Seek out mentorship or guidance from experienced real estate professionals who have a proven track record of providing exceptional customer service. Learn from their experiences and apply their strategies and techniques to your own business.

5. Utilize Technology and Tools: Embrace technology and leverage tools that can streamline your processes and enhance your customer service efforts. Use customer relationship management (CRM) software to manage client interactions, automate follow-ups, and stay organized.

6. Develop Strong Communication Skills: Continuously work on improving your communication skills, both verbal and written. Clear and effective communication is essential for building trust, understanding client needs, and addressing concerns promptly.

7. Stay Engaged with Your Clients: Even after a transaction is complete, maintain regular contact with your clients. Send personalized emails, make phone calls, or connect through social media to stay engaged and show that you value the relationship beyond the transaction.

Developing expertise in providing exceptional customer service is a continuous journey. By embracing a growth mindset, seeking professional development opportunities, staying informed, learning from experienced professionals, utilizing technology, honing communication skills, and staying engaged with your clients, you can continuously enhance your customer service and stand out in the real estate industry.

Remember, exceptional customer service not only benefits your business financially but also enriches the lives of your clients. By providing top-notch service, you create memorable experiences, build trust, and establish long-lasting relationships. Your commitment to exceptional customer service will set you apart from the competition and position you as the go-to real estate professional in your market.

Let's delve deeper into the steps involved in providing outstanding customer service throughout the buying or selling process:

1. Establish Rapport and Build Trust: From the initial contact, focus on building a genuine connection with your clients. Take the time to understand their goals, concerns, and preferences. Show empathy, actively listen, and demonstrate your expertise to instill confidence and trust in your abilities.

2. Educate and Inform: Help your clients navigate the real estate process by providing them with comprehensive and accurate information. Explain the steps involved, answer their questions promptly, and address any concerns they may have. Keep them informed about market trends, property updates, and important deadlines.

3. Personalize the Experience: Tailor your approach to each client's unique needs and preferences. Take note of their specific requirements and provide personalized recommendations and options that align with their goals. Going the extra mile to make them feel seen and valued will leave a lasting impression.

4. Provide Timely and Transparent Communication: Communication is the backbone of exceptional customer service. Keep your clients informed at every stage of the process, ensuring they are aware of progress, any potential challenges, and next steps. Be proactive in reaching out and promptly respond to their calls, emails, or messages.

5. Offer Guidance and Expert Advice: As a real estate professional, your expertise is invaluable. Guide your clients through the decision-making process by providing objective advice, market insights, and potential risks or opportunities they should consider. Help them make informed decisions that align with their best interests.

6. Coordinate and Facilitate Smooth Transactions: Take charge of coordinating the various aspects of the transaction, such as scheduling inspections, negotiating offers, and liaising with

other parties involved. Act as a facilitator to ensure a seamless and efficient process, minimizing stress for your clients.

7. Anticipate and Solve Problems: Real estate transactions can be complex, and challenges may arise along the way. Stay proactive in identifying potential obstacles and finding solutions to overcome them. Your ability to anticipate and navigate hurdles demonstrates your commitment to delivering exceptional customer service.

8. Provide Post-Transaction Support: Your relationship with clients doesn't end when the deal is closed. Follow up with them after the transaction to ensure they are satisfied with their purchase or sale. Offer assistance with any post-transaction needs, such as recommending service providers or helping with property-related inquiries.

9. Request Feedback and Learn from it: Continuously seek feedback from your clients to understand their experience working with you. Feedback provides valuable insights for improvement and helps you refine your customer service approach. Use feedback as an opportunity to learn, grow, and enhance your services.

10. Foster Long-Term Relationships: Building strong, long-term relationships is the key to repeat business and referrals. Stay in touch with past clients through newsletters, holiday greetings, or personalized updates. Maintain a database of client information, preferences, and milestones to ensure personalized interactions.

By following these steps and consistently delivering exceptional customer service, you not only enhance your clients' experience but also strengthen your reputation as a reliable and trusted real estate professional. Word-of-mouth referrals and repeat business will naturally follow, further fueling your success in the industry. Remember, going above and beyond for your clients is not only a smart business strategy but also a reflection of your genuine commitment to their success and satisfaction.

Going above and beyond for your clients is not just a nice gesture, it's a necessary aspect of providing exceptional customer service.

When you make the extra effort to exceed your clients' expectations, you are not only providing them with a memorable experience, but also building a loyal client base and increasing the chances of receiving referrals in the future. Here are some strategies for going above and beyond:

1. Be proactive: Anticipate your clients' needs and address them before they even have to ask. For example, if you know they are moving to a new area, provide them with a list of recommended restaurants, schools, and other resources in the area.
2. Be available: Make yourself available to your clients whenever they need you, even if it means working outside of traditional business hours. Answer their calls and emails promptly and make sure they feel like they are a priority.
3. Personalize the experience: Get to know your clients on a personal level and tailor your services to their unique needs and preferences. Remember important details about their family, interests, and lifestyle, and use this information to provide personalized recommendations and advice.
4. Follow up: Don't just close a deal and forget about your clients. Follow up after the sale to make sure they are satisfied with their experience and to address any additional needs they may have.
5. Surprise and delight: Go the extra mile to surprise your clients with thoughtful gestures, such as sending a personalized gift or handwritten note to congratulate them on their new home purchase.

When you make the extra effort to exceed your clients' expectations, you are not only providing them with exceptional customer service, but also setting yourself apart from other realtors in the industry. By consistently going above and beyond, you will establish a reputation as a trusted and reliable realtor who truly cares about their clients' needs and success.

Here's some additional depth and insight on why going above and beyond is the only way you should ever consider doing business:

1. Building trust and loyalty: By exceeding your clients' expectations, you are building trust and fostering a sense of loyalty. When clients see that you are willing to go the extra mile for them, they will feel more confident in your abilities and will be more likely to refer you to their friends, family, and colleagues.
2. Differentiating yourself from the competition: In a competitive real estate market, providing exceptional customer service sets you apart from the competition. Many realtors may offer similar services, but by going above and beyond, you create a memorable experience that clients will remember and appreciate.
3. Generating positive word-of-mouth: Happy clients are more likely to share their positive experiences with others. By providing exceptional customer service, you are increasing the chances of receiving positive word-of-mouth referrals. This can lead to a steady stream of new clients and a stronger network within your community.
4. Building long-term relationships: Real estate is not just about one-time transactions; it's about building relationships. When you consistently provide exceptional customer service, you are more likely to build long-term relationships with your clients. This means that they will come back to you for future real estate needs and will refer you to others.
5. Enhancing your professional reputation: Your reputation as a realtor is crucial to your success. By going above and beyond, you enhance your professional reputation and establish yourself as a trusted expert in the industry. This can lead to more opportunities, partnerships, and referrals from other professionals.
6. Increasing client satisfaction and happiness: At the end of the day, exceptional customer service is about ensuring your clients' satisfaction and happiness. When you go above and beyond, you are showing that you genuinely care about their needs and are committed to helping them achieve their real estate goals. This not only leads to a more positive experience

for your clients, but it also brings you personal fulfillment and a sense of pride in your work.

Remember, providing exceptional customer service is not just a one-time effort, but a consistent commitment throughout the entire client journey. By consistently going above and beyond, you create a reputation for excellence and establish yourself as a realtor who is dedicated to delivering outstanding results and client satisfaction.

Here's some additional depth and insight on the best and proven strategies for going above and beyond to exceed client expectations:

1. Anticipate their needs: One of the keys to providing exceptional customer service is to anticipate your clients' needs before they even express them. Take the time to listen attentively and understand their goals, preferences, and concerns. By proactively addressing their needs and offering personalized solutions, you demonstrate your commitment to their success and satisfaction.

2. Provide regular communication: Communication is essential in the real estate process, and keeping your clients informed and updated is crucial. Establish a regular communication schedule and be responsive to their inquiries and concerns. This can be through phone calls, emails, or even text messages. By keeping them informed about the progress of their transaction and promptly addressing any questions or issues, you build trust and confidence in your service.

3. Offer valuable resources and guidance: As a realtor, you have extensive knowledge and expertise in the real estate market. Share this knowledge with your clients by providing them with valuable resources, such as market reports, neighborhood guides, or home buying/selling tips. Educate them about the process and offer guidance to help them make informed decisions. By providing valuable information and guidance, you position yourself as a trusted advisor and resource.

4. Personalize the experience: Every client is unique, and tailoring your approach to their individual needs and preferences can make a significant impact. Take the time to

understand their motivations, lifestyle, and priorities. Offer personalized recommendations and solutions that align with their specific situation. This personal touch shows that you genuinely care about their success and are willing to go the extra mile to meet their expectations.

5. Offer additional services or support: Consider going beyond the traditional scope of a realtor's duties by offering additional services or support. This can include connecting them with trusted professionals, such as mortgage brokers, home inspectors, or interior designers. You can also assist with arranging moving services, providing local recommendations, or even helping them with post-move follow-ups. By providing these extra touches, you demonstrate your commitment to their overall satisfaction and create a memorable experience.

6. Follow up after the transaction: Exceptional customer service doesn't end with the closing of a deal. Follow up with your clients after the transaction to ensure their continued satisfaction. This can be a simple phone call or email to check in, ask for feedback, and address any lingering questions or concerns. By maintaining a relationship with past clients, you increase the likelihood of repeat business and referrals.

Providing exceptional customer service requires a genuine commitment to your clients' success and satisfaction. It's about going above and beyond their expectations and consistently delivering outstanding results. By incorporating these strategies into your business approach, you not only differentiate yourself from the competition but also build long-term relationships and a stellar reputation as a realtor who consistently exceeds client expectations.

There are numerous brands that are known for providing exceptional customer service. These brands have developed a reputation for going above and beyond to meet their customers' needs and exceed their expectations. They understand that providing exceptional customer service is the key to creating a loyal customer base and establishing themselves as a leader in their industry.

One example of such a brand is Nordstrom. This department store is famous for its exceptional customer service. They offer free shipping and returns, personal shopping services, and even alterations. Nordstrom understands the importance of creating a positive customer experience, and they consistently strive to exceed their customers' expectations.

Another example is Zappos, an online retailer of shoes and clothing. They have become known for their commitment to customer service, offering free shipping and returns, a 365-day return policy, and 24/7 customer support. Zappos also takes a unique approach to hiring, focusing on hiring individuals who are passionate about providing excellent customer service, and they invest in training to ensure their employees are well-equipped to serve their customers.

Amazon is another brand that has developed a reputation for providing exceptional customer service. They offer a wide selection of products, competitive prices, and fast shipping. They also have a robust customer support system, including a 24/7 customer service hotline and an extensive knowledge base. Amazon's customer-centric approach has helped them become one of the largest and most successful companies in the world.

These brands are successful because they understand the importance of providing exceptional customer service. They go above and beyond to meet their customers' needs, and they prioritize creating a positive customer experience. By doing so, they have created a loyal customer base that is eager to return and recommend their services to others.

As a real estate professional, it's essential to adopt a similar approach to customer service. By prioritizing the needs of your clients and going above and beyond to exceed their expectations, you will establish yourself as a trusted advisor and create a loyal client base. This means not only providing exceptional service during the buying or selling process but also after the transaction is complete. Following up with clients, providing valuable resources and information, and continuing to build a relationship with them are all ways to ensure you are providing exceptional customer service.

In summary, providing exceptional customer service is vital to the longevity and success of any business. By studying successful brands that prioritize customer service, adopting proven strategies, and going above and beyond to exceed client expectations, you can build a reputation as a trusted advisor and create a loyal client base that will contribute to the growth of your business.

Continuing on the topic of providing exceptional customer service, it's important to understand why going above and beyond is the only way you should ever consider doing business. Exceptional customer service not only sets you apart from your competitors, but it also builds trust, fosters loyalty, and generates positive word-of-mouth referrals. When you consistently go the extra mile for your clients, you create memorable experiences that leave a lasting impression.

One of the key benefits of going above and beyond is the establishment of trust. When clients see that you genuinely care about their needs and are willing to go the extra mile to meet them, it builds trust and confidence in your abilities. They feel reassured that you have their best interests at heart and that you will do whatever it takes to ensure their satisfaction. Trust is the foundation of any successful relationship, and by providing exceptional customer service, you strengthen that foundation.

Another advantage of exceeding expectations is the creation of loyalty. Clients who experience outstanding service are more likely to become repeat customers and refer you to others. They appreciate the value you bring to the table and the effort you put into making their experience exceptional. By consistently providing exceptional customer service, you cultivate a loyal following of clients who become advocates for your business. They become your brand ambassadors, spreading positive word-of-mouth and helping you attract new clients organically.

Furthermore, going above and beyond allows you to differentiate yourself in a crowded marketplace. With so many real estate professionals competing for clients, providing exceptional customer service sets you apart as someone who truly cares and delivers results. Clients will remember the extra attention, personalized touches, and efforts you made to make their experience memorable. This differentiation helps you stand out from the competition and positions you as a trusted expert in your field.

To illustrate the impact of exceptional customer service, let's look at an example from the hospitality industry. The Ritz-Carlton is known for its legendary customer service, and it's a prime example of a brand that goes above and beyond to create exceptional experiences. One of their famous stories involves a family who stayed at the hotel and left behind their son's beloved stuffed giraffe. The staff at the Ritz-Carlton went out of their way to locate the giraffe, took pictures of it "enjoying" various hotel activities, and sent the photos to the family. This thoughtful gesture not only delighted the family but also created a memorable experience that they shared with others. It's stories like these that showcase the power of exceptional customer service in building lasting relationships and generating positive referrals.

In the real estate industry, going above and beyond may involve personalized home search strategies, offering additional resources and guidance, or even providing assistance with post-transaction needs. It's about anticipating and exceeding client expectations at every stage of the buying or selling process. By doing so, you demonstrate your commitment to exceptional customer service and create a positive reputation that will attract future clients.

Remember providing exceptional customer service is not just a nice-to-have but an essential component of a successful real estate business. Going above and beyond for your clients builds trust, fosters loyalty, differentiates you from competitors, and generates positive word-of-mouth referrals. By consistently striving to exceed expectations, you create memorable experiences that leave a lasting impression on your clients. Remember, exceptional customer service is not just a transactional approach; it's a mindset and a commitment to delivering excellence in every interaction.

Trust is a crucial factor in any business relationship, and the real estate industry is no exception. Providing exceptional customer service is the foundation for building trust with your clients, which is essential for developing long-term business relationships. When clients feel that their needs are being heard and taken care of, they are more likely to trust you as a professional and feel comfortable with you guiding them through the buying or selling process.

Trust is not just about delivering on your promises; it's about going above and beyond to exceed your client's expectations. It's about being honest, transparent, and demonstrating a genuine interest in their success. When you consistently provide exceptional customer service, your clients will come to trust you implicitly, knowing that you have their best interests at heart.

Building trust with your clients starts with active listening, which is one of the key components of exceptional customer service. By listening to your clients' needs, you can tailor your services to their specific goals and create a personalized approach that will resonate with them. Additionally, following through on commitments, being transparent with information, and being responsive to their concerns and questions are all crucial elements that contribute to building trust.

Real estate agents who have established a reputation for providing exceptional customer service build a loyal client base that comes back to them for repeat business and referrals. These clients become advocates for the agent and will refer their friends and family to them, ultimately driving more business. In today's digital age, online reviews and ratings also play a significant role in building trust with potential clients. Positive reviews and testimonials from satisfied clients can help establish an agent's reputation and credibility, making it easier to build trust with new clients.

In conclusion, trust is an essential byproduct of providing exceptional customer service. When clients trust you, they are more likely to feel comfortable with you guiding them through the buying or selling process, leading to more successful transactions and repeat business. By actively listening to your clients, following through on commitments, and going above and beyond to exceed their expectations, you can build trust and establish a solid foundation for your real estate business.

CHAPTER 5: NETWORKING AND COMMUNITY INVOLVEMENT - BUILDING STRONG CONNECTIONS AND MAKING A POSITIVE IMPACT

Networking and community involvement are two powerful tools that can greatly enhance your success as a real estate professional. In this chapter, we will explore the benefits of networking and being involved in the community, and provide you with actionable steps to effectively build strong connections and make a positive impact. By actively engaging with others and contributing to your community, you can expand your professional network, gain valuable referrals, and establish yourself as a trusted authority in the real estate industry.

The Power of Networking

1. Building Relationships: Networking allows you to connect with other professionals in your industry, such as fellow real estate agents, mortgage brokers, and home inspectors. By

building relationships with these individuals, you can establish a network of trusted colleagues who can provide support, advice, and potential business opportunities.

2. Referral Opportunities: Networking opens the door to referral opportunities. When you develop strong relationships with professionals in related fields, they are more likely to refer their clients to you when they need real estate services. This can lead to a steady stream of referrals, which is a valuable source of new business.

3. Industry Insights and Knowledge: Through networking, you have the opportunity to learn from others who have extensive experience in the real estate industry. Attending industry events, conferences, and seminars can provide valuable insights and keep you updated on the latest trends and developments in the market.

The Benefits of Community Involvement

1. Establishing Trust and Credibility: Being actively involved in your community demonstrates your commitment and dedication to making a positive impact. When people see you participating in local events, volunteering, or supporting community initiatives, it enhances your reputation and establishes trust and credibility with potential clients. They are more likely to choose you as their real estate agent because they see you as someone who cares about the community and can be trusted to serve their best interests.

2. Expanding Your Network: Community involvement provides ample opportunities to meet new people and expand your professional network. Whether it's participating in local business associations, attending community meetings, or volunteering for charitable organizations, you have the chance to connect with individuals from various backgrounds and industries. These connections can lead to referrals, partnerships, and collaborative opportunities that can benefit your real estate business.

3. Deepening Local Market Knowledge: Being involved in your community gives you a deeper understanding of the local market. You become more aware of the unique needs, preferences, and challenges of the residents. This knowledge allows you to tailor your services and marketing efforts to better serve the community and attract potential clients who resonate with your understanding of their specific needs.

Actionable Steps for Networking and Community Involvement

1. Attend Industry Events: Make it a priority to attend industry conferences, trade shows, and networking events. Engage in conversations, exchange business cards, and follow up with the individuals you meet to nurture those connections.
2. Join Professional Associations: Join local and national real estate associations to connect with other professionals in your field. Attend their meetings, participate in committees, and take advantage of the educational and networking opportunities they offer.
3. Volunteer in the Community: Identify organizations or causes that align with your values and interests, and volunteer your time and expertise. This not only allows you to give back but also puts you in contact with like-minded individuals who may become potential clients or referral sources.
4. Sponsor Local Events: Consider sponsoring local events, such as charity fundraisers, sports teams, or community festivals. This not only increases your visibility but also demonstrates your commitment to supporting the community.
5. Collaborate with Local Businesses: Build relationships with other local businesses that complement your services, such as mortgage brokers, home builders, or interior designers. Partnering with these professionals can lead to cross-referrals and collaborative marketing efforts.

Networking and community involvement are essential for building strong connections, gaining referrals, and establishing trust and credibility in the real estate industry. By actively engaging with others and making a positive impact in your community, you can expand your professional network, deepen your market knowledge, and attract clients who value your commitment to serving their needs. Embrace the power of networking and community involvement, and watch your real estate business thrive.

We will delve into the strategies for building a strong network of industry contacts and the importance of keeping up with these contacts. Networking is not just about making initial connections; it's about nurturing and maintaining those relationships over time. By actively engaging with industry contacts, you can create a robust network that supports your real estate business and opens doors to new opportunities. Let's explore the step-by-step process and the benefits of staying connected.

Building a Strong Network

1. Define Your Objectives: Start by defining your networking objectives. Determine what you hope to achieve through your network, whether it's generating referrals, gaining industry insights, or forming partnerships. Having a clear goal will guide your networking efforts and help you focus on building relationships that align with your objectives.

2. Attend Industry Events: Industry events, conferences, and seminars provide excellent opportunities to connect with professionals in your field. Be proactive in attending these events, engaging in conversations, and exchanging contact information. Remember to follow up with the individuals you meet to nurture those connections and explore potential collaborations.

3. Join Professional Associations: Joining professional associations in the real estate industry allows you to connect with like-minded individuals and access valuable resources. Attend association meetings, participate in committees, and take advantage of networking events organized by these associations. Building relationships within these organizations can lead to fruitful connections and referrals.

4. Utilize Online Networking Platforms: In addition to in-person networking, leverage online networking platforms such as LinkedIn

to expand your reach. Connect with other real estate professionals, join industry-specific groups, and engage in discussions. Actively share valuable content and insights to position yourself as a knowledgeable and helpful resource within the online community.

Importance of Keeping in Touch

1. Nurture Relationships: Building a network is not a one-time task; it requires consistent effort to nurture and maintain relationships. Regularly reach out to your industry contacts, congratulate them on their achievements, and inquire about their current projects. Showing genuine interest in their endeavors helps strengthen the bond and encourages reciprocity.

2. Stay Updated with Industry News: Keeping up with industry news and trends allows you to engage in meaningful conversations with your contacts. Share relevant articles or insights and seek their opinions. This demonstrates your commitment to staying informed and positions you as a trusted source of industry knowledge.

3. Provide Value: One of the best ways to maintain strong relationships is by providing value to your contacts. Share useful resources, such as market reports, tips for homebuyers or sellers, or referrals to trusted service providers. By consistently offering value, you become a valuable asset in your contacts' network, and they are more likely to reciprocate by referring clients or sharing opportunities with you.

4. Personalize Communication: Tailor your communication to each contact, making it personal and genuine. Remember key details about their interests, challenges, or milestones, and reference them in your conversations. This shows that you genuinely care about their well-being and fosters a deeper connection.

Benefits of a Strong Network

1. Referral Opportunities: A strong network increases the likelihood of receiving referrals from industry contacts. When someone in your network comes across a client who needs real estate services, they

are more likely to recommend you if you have built a strong relationship and consistently provided value.

2. Collaborative Opportunities: Building a network of industry contacts opens doors to collaborative opportunities. You may find opportunities to partner with other professionals on joint marketing campaigns, share leads, or collaborate on projects. These collaborations can expand your reach and help you tap into new markets.

3. Industry Insights and Learning: By staying connected with industry contacts, you gain access to valuable industry insights and learning opportunities.

Your network can serve as a platform for sharing best practices, discussing market trends, and seeking advice from experienced professionals. This continuous learning keeps you informed and helps you adapt to industry changes.

4. Personal and Professional Growth: Building a strong network not only benefits your business but also contributes to personal and professional growth. Engaging with industry peers, mentors, and thought leaders exposes you to diverse perspectives, challenges your assumptions, and helps you develop new skills. The knowledge and experiences gained through networking can enhance your expertise and position you as a leader in your field.

Networking and community involvement are vital for building a successful real estate business. By following the strategies outlined in this chapter and maintaining strong connections, you can expand your network, create meaningful relationships, and access a wealth of opportunities. Remember, networking is not just about what you can gain; it's about building mutually beneficial relationships and contributing to the growth and success of others in your industry. Embrace the power of networking and community involvement, and watch your real estate business thrive.

Strategies for Building a Strong Network of Industry Contacts

1. Follow Up and Follow Through: After meeting new contacts at events or through online platforms, it's essential to follow up promptly. Send personalized emails or messages expressing your pleasure in meeting them and referencing something from your conversation. This shows your sincerity and helps solidify the connection. Additionally, make it a priority to follow through on any promises or commitments you made during your interactions. This demonstrates reliability and builds trust.

2. Cultivate Relationships with Influencers: Identify influential individuals in your industry and make an effort to connect with them. These influencers could be established real estate professionals, successful investors, or respected thought leaders. Engage with their content, attend their presentations or webinars, and reach out to them with thoughtful comments or questions. Building a relationship with influencers can open doors to valuable connections and opportunities.

3. Attend Local Business Events: Networking is not limited to industry-specific events. Attend local business events, chamber of commerce meetings, or community gatherings where you can meet professionals from diverse fields. Building relationships with individuals outside the real estate industry can lead to referrals, partnerships, and cross-promotional opportunities.

4. Provide Value to Others: Building a strong network is not just about what you can gain; it's also about what you can offer. Look for opportunities to provide value to your contacts by sharing your expertise, offering advice, or making introductions. Actively listen to their needs and challenges and seek ways to support them. When you consistently provide value, you become a valuable resource and someone they will turn to when they need assistance.

5. Participate in Industry Forums and Groups: Join online forums, discussion groups, or social media communities focused on real estate or specific niches within the industry. Actively participate by sharing your insights, answering questions, and engaging in discussions. This not only positions you as an expert but also helps

you connect with like-minded professionals who share similar interests and challenges.

6. Host or Speak at Industry Events: Take the initiative to host or speak at industry events, seminars, or webinars. This positions you as a knowledgeable authority in your field and provides an opportunity to showcase your expertise to a larger audience. By sharing valuable insights and practical tips, you establish yourself as a go-to resource, attracting the attention of potential clients and industry peers.

7. Leverage Social Media: Social media platforms such as LinkedIn, Twitter, and Facebook offer powerful tools for building and maintaining your network. Regularly post industry-related content, share success stories, and engage with your connections by commenting on their posts or initiating conversations. Use social media as a platform to showcase your expertise, connect with industry influencers, and expand your reach to a wider audience.

8. Attend Training and Development Programs: Stay updated with industry trends and enhance your skills by attending training programs, workshops, or conferences. These events not only provide valuable knowledge but also offer networking opportunities with other participants and industry experts. Engaging with like-minded professionals who are also focused on personal and professional development can lead to long-lasting connections and collaborations.

Building a strong network of industry contacts requires consistent effort, genuine engagement, and a focus on mutual value creation. By following the strategies outlined in this chapter, you can establish meaningful connections, access new opportunities, and stay at the forefront of your industry. Remember that networking is a continuous process, and it's important to nurture and maintain your relationships over time. Embrace the power of networking and community involvement, and watch as your real estate business thrives with the support and collaboration of a strong network.

Maximizing Online Presence and Community Engagement

By actively participating in community events, engaging with local organizations, and maximizing your online presence, you can build a strong brand and generate business opportunities. Community involvement not only helps you establish meaningful connections with potential clients but also positions you as a trusted and engaged professional in your area. Through networking, collaborating with local businesses, and providing valuable content, you create a positive impact on your community while building a loyal client base. Embrace the power of community engagement, both online and offline, and watch as your reputation and business thrive in the real estate industry.

1. Leverage Social Media: Use social media platforms to extend your community involvement and build your brand online. Share updates about your participation in community events, highlight local organizations, and engage with followers. Use platforms like Facebook, Instagram, and Twitter to share valuable content, such as tips for homebuyers or local market updates. By actively engaging with your online audience, you can further establish your expertise and connect with potential clients.

2. Create Community-Centric Content: Develop content that resonates with your community and showcases your knowledge and expertise. This could include blog posts, videos, or podcasts that address local real estate trends, neighborhood spotlights, or homeowner tips. By creating content that is relevant and valuable to your target audience, you position yourself as a go-to resource for real estate information in your community.

3. Participate in Online Groups and Forums: Engage in online forums and groups where community members discuss local events, real estate topics, and homeowner concerns. Actively contribute to these discussions by sharing insights, answering questions, and providing helpful resources. By being a valuable participant in these online communities, you build credibility and gain visibility among potential clients.

4. Collaborate with Local Businesses: Strengthen your community engagement by collaborating with local businesses and

professionals. Identify complementary businesses such as mortgage brokers, home inspectors, or interior designers, and explore opportunities for joint marketing efforts or referral partnerships. By working together, you can amplify your reach, support local businesses, and provide a comprehensive network of services to your clients.

5. Measure and Adapt: Regularly evaluate the effectiveness of your community involvement and online engagement strategies. Monitor the impact of your efforts by tracking metrics such as website traffic, social media engagement, and lead generation. Use these insights to make informed adjustments to your approach and focus on activities that yield the best results. Continually refine your strategies to ensure they align with the evolving needs and preferences of your target audience.

6. Sponsor Local Events: Consider sponsoring local events that align with your target audience and values. This could be a charity fundraiser, a community festival, or a youth sports team. By becoming a sponsor, you not only support the community but also gain visibility and recognition as a local real estate expert. Your brand will be associated with positive experiences and community goodwill, enhancing your reputation and attracting potential clients.

7. Volunteer in the Community: Look for volunteer opportunities within your community that allow you to contribute your time and skills. This could involve serving on a local committee, participating in community clean-up initiatives, or mentoring aspiring homeowners. By giving back, you demonstrate your commitment to the community's well-being and create a positive impression in the minds of residents. This can lead to referrals and word-of-mouth recommendations as people recognize your dedication and genuine interest in the community.

8. Attend Local Networking Events: Stay active in your industry by attending local networking events, conferences, and trade shows. These events provide valuable opportunities to connect with fellow professionals, exchange ideas, and learn about the latest trends and developments in the real estate market. Actively participate in

discussions, share insights, and make genuine connections. Networking events can lead to collaborations, referrals, and valuable partnerships that benefit your business in the long run.

9. Engage with Local Media: Build relationships with local media outlets, including newspapers, magazines, and radio stations. Offer yourself as a resource for real estate expertise and be available for interviews or expert commentary on relevant topics. Contributing to local publications or hosting a radio show can position you as a knowledgeable authority in your field and help you reach a broader audience. This exposure increases your visibility and credibility within the community and can generate leads and referrals.

10. Stay Informed: Continuously educate yourself about local market trends, changes in real estate laws, and emerging technologies in the industry. Attend seminars, workshops, and webinars to stay updated and enhance your knowledge base. By staying informed, you can provide accurate and valuable advice to your clients, positioning yourself as a trusted advisor. This commitment to ongoing learning demonstrates your dedication to excellence and further establishes your expertise in the eyes of potential clients.

11. Foster Long-Term Relationships: Building strong relationships with clients goes beyond the transactional aspect of real estate. Maintain regular communication with past and current clients, even after the deal is closed. Send personalized follow-up emails, make occasional phone calls, or send small tokens of appreciation on special occasions. By nurturing these relationships, you build loyalty and create brand ambassadors who will refer you to their friends, family, and colleagues.

12. Seek Feedback and Continuously Improve: Actively seek feedback from your clients about their experience working with you. Listen to their suggestions and use their feedback to improve your processes and customer service. Implementing changes based on client feedback shows your commitment to continuous improvement and client satisfaction. By addressing concerns and exceeding expectations, you demonstrate that you value your clients and their opinions, fostering long-term trust and loyalty.

By providing exceptional customer service involves actively engaging in networking and community involvement. By participating in local events, sponsoring initiatives, volunteering, and networking with industry professionals, you position yourself as an active and invested member of your community. Additionally, staying informed, engaging with local media, and fostering long-term relationships contribute to building your reputation and generating business opportunities. By consistently going above and beyond for your clients and the community, you create a memorable and positive experience that sets you apart from your competitors. The result is a thriving real estate business with a loyal client base and a respected position within your community.

CHAPTER 6: RECAP

Chapter 1: Building a Repeat Business
In Chapter 1, we explored the importance of building a repeat business and generating referrals. We discussed how providing exceptional service, staying in touch, showcasing expertise, using social media, and partnering with other professionals can all contribute to building a loyal client base. We emphasized the need to be persistent but not obnoxious in asking for referrals and the power of persistence in the long run. By implementing these strategies, real estate professionals can create a strong foundation for their business and establish themselves as trusted experts in their field.

Chapter 2: Marketing and Branding
In Chapter 2, we delved into the world of marketing and branding. We highlighted the significance of a strong brand in standing out in a crowded market and attracting clients. We explored strategies for building a memorable brand through a distinctive logo and catchy tagline. Consistency in messaging, both online and offline, was emphasized as a way to build trust and familiarity with the brand. We discussed the importance of understanding the target audience and tailoring marketing strategies to effectively reach and connect with them. We also touched upon the importance of a user-friendly website and the power of social media in building a strong brand presence.

Chapter 3: Developing Expertise
Chapter 3 focused on the development of expertise in a specific niche. We explored the benefits of specializing in a particular area and discussed strategies for becoming an expert, such as seeking mentorship, continuing education, and limiting the client pool. We emphasized the importance of positioning oneself as an expert in the chosen niche to attract clients who value specialized knowledge and experience. Developing expertise not only benefits the real estate

professional financially but also ensures that clients receive top-notch service tailored to their specific needs.

Chapter 4: Providing Exceptional Customer Service

Chapter 4 highlighted the crucial role of exceptional customer service in the success and longevity of a realtor's career. We discussed the importance of active listening, responsiveness, and empathy in understanding and addressing clients' needs and concerns. We provided step-by-step guidance on providing outstanding customer service throughout the buying or selling process, from the initial consultation to post-transaction follow-up. We emphasized the significance of going above and beyond to exceed client expectations and create a memorable experience. Trust was identified as a byproduct of exceptional customer service, fostering long-term client relationships and generating referrals.

Chapter 5: Networking and Community Involvement

In Chapter 5, we explored the benefits of networking and community involvement for real estate professionals. We discussed strategies for building a strong network of industry contacts and the importance of maintaining those relationships. We highlighted the value of attending networking events, engaging with professional associations, and staying up-to-date with industry contacts. Additionally, we explored how getting involved in community events and organizations can build brand visibility and generate business. Sponsoring local events, volunteering, and engaging with local media were identified as effective ways to establish oneself as a trusted authority and gain community recognition.

Building a successful career in real estate requires a comprehensive approach that encompasses exceptional customer service, effective marketing and branding, expertise in a specific niche, and active networking and community involvement. By implementing the strategies outlined in this guide, aspiring real estate professionals can create a solid foundation for their business and stand out in a competitive market.

Key Strategies for Building a Repeat Business and Standing Out as a Realtor:

1. Provide exceptional customer service by actively listening, being responsive, and going above and beyond to exceed client expectations.
2. Develop a strong brand through a memorable logo, consistent messaging, and effective online and offline marketing strategies.
3. Specialize in a specific niche to become an expert in that area and attract clients seeking specialized knowledge and experience.
4. Engage in networking activities and community involvement to build a strong network of industry contacts and establish yourself as a trusted authority in the community.
5. Foster long-term client relationships by staying in touch, providing personalized follow-up, and seeking feedback for continuous improvement.
6. Stay informed and up-to-date on industry trends and changes through ongoing education, attending seminars, and networking with professionals.
7. Build trust through exceptional customer service, reliability, and consistently delivering on promises.
8. Seek out mentorship and learn from experienced professionals in the industry.
9. Embrace technology and utilize digital tools to streamline processes, enhance communication, and provide a seamless client experience.
10. Stay positive, persistent, and resilient in the face of challenges and setbacks.

Final Thoughts and Advice for Aspiring Real Estate Professionals:

Becoming a successful real estate professional requires dedication, hard work, and a commitment to providing exceptional service. It is essential to prioritize building relationships, understanding clients' needs, and constantly striving for excellence. By developing expertise, building a strong brand, and actively engaging with the community, you can stand out in a crowded market and build a thriving business. Remember, providing exceptional customer service is not just about financial gains but also about making a positive impact on people's lives during one of the most significant decisions they will make. By focusing on building trust, exceeding expectations, and delivering top-notch client service, you will not only achieve professional success but also enjoy a fulfilling and rewarding career in real estate.

The journey to building a successful career as a real estate professional is multifaceted and requires a combination of skills, strategies, and a commitment to providing exceptional customer service. By following the key strategies outlined in this guide, you can differentiate yourself from the competition, cultivate a loyal client base, and position yourself as a trusted expert in your field.

Remember that exceptional customer service is the foundation of your business. By actively listening to your clients' needs and concerns, you can gain a deep understanding of their goals and tailor your services to meet their unique requirements. Going above and beyond their expectations not only creates a memorable experience but also builds trust and fosters long-term relationships. Happy clients become loyal advocates who are more likely to refer you to their friends, family, and colleagues.

Developing expertise in a specific niche is another crucial aspect of your success. By specializing in a particular area, such as luxury homes, first-time buyers, probate, or seller-only transactions, you can become the go-to expert in that market segment. This specialized knowledge and experience will attract clients seeking your expertise, and they will trust that you can deliver the best results for their specific needs.

Continuing education is vital to stay current in the ever-evolving real estate industry. Take advantage of seminars, workshops, webinars, and industry conferences to stay informed about the latest trends, regulations, and technologies. This ongoing learning will enhance your skills, broaden your knowledge base, and demonstrate to clients that you are committed to providing the highest level of service.

Networking and community involvement are essential components of your success as a realtor. Building a strong network of industry contacts allows you to tap into valuable resources, gain insights from experienced professionals, and receive referrals. Actively participate in networking events, engage with professional associations, and maintain relationships with colleagues and peers in the industry. Additionally, getting involved in community events and organizations not only helps raise your visibility but also showcases your commitment to the community and builds trust among potential clients.

In summary, the real estate profession demands a combination of expertise, exceptional customer service, effective marketing and branding, networking, and community involvement. By focusing on these key areas, you can build a solid foundation for your business, cultivate a loyal client base, and enjoy a successful and fulfilling career. Remember to always prioritize the needs of your clients, go above and beyond their expectations, and continuously strive for excellence. By doing so, you will not only achieve financial success but also create meaningful and lasting relationships with your clients. Embrace the journey, stay committed to personal growth, and embrace the opportunities that come your way. Good luck on your path to becoming a highly respected and successful real estate professional!

ABOUT THE AUTHOR

Kwame Joseph

Kwame Joseph is a licensed realtor with over 10 years of experience in the real estate industry. He has won numerous awards for his exceptional work in the field and has become a respected name in the industry. Born in Georgetown, Guyana, Kwame immigrated to the United States at the age of 8. Throughout his life, he has faced many challenges, but he has always been determined to succeed.

BOOKS BY THIS AUTHOR

Navigating The Rental Property Market: A handbook for Investors

"Navigating the Rental Property Market: A Handbook for Investors" is a comprehensive and informative book that covers all aspects of real estate investing, from the basics of property acquisition and financing to advanced strategies for maximizing profits and minimizing risk. This guide explores the different types of real estate investments, the pros and cons of each, and the strategies and techniques that can help investors make smart, informed decisions. With practical tips and expert advice, this book is perfect for both beginners just starting out and experienced investors looking to take their business to the next level. Whether you're interested in residential or commercial properties, vacation properties, or land investments, this guide has something for everyone.

From Data to Dollars: Using AI to Monetize Your Business: The Benefits of AI for Monetization.

"From Data to Dollars: Using AI to Monetize Your Businesss" is a comprehensive guide for business owners, entrepreneurs, and executives looking to leverage the power of AI for their companies. The book covers a wide range of topics, from understanding the basics of AI to monetizing its applications. It features case studies of successful AI implementations, as well as detailed analyses of the ethical and regulatory considerations surrounding AI. The book also explores emerging technologies and trends that are likely to shape the future of AI monetization. With actionable steps for implementing AI in business and a user-friendly narrative tone, "AI Monetization" is an essential resource for anyone looking to stay ahead of the curve in the world of business and technology.

First-Time Homebuyer's Guide: A Comprehensive Handbook

"First-Time Homebuyer's Guide: A Comprehensive Handbook" is a step-by-step guide that walks readers through the entire process of buying a home for the first time. From preparing to buy a home to moving in and maintaining it, this guide covers everything first-time homebuyers need to know. It includes information on understanding the homebuying process, determining your budget and financing options, finding the right property, making an offer and negotiating the sale, securing a mortgage and closing the sale, and more. This handbook also provides tips and resources to help readers avoid common mistakes that first-time homebuyers can make. Whether you're a first-time homebuyer or just looking to refresh your knowledge of the homebuying process, this guide is a valuable resource for anyone looking to purchase a home.

www.ingramcontent.com/pod-product-compliance
Lightning Source LLC
Chambersburg PA
CBHW070448220526
45466CB00004B/1781